D1525745

North Carolina
Parade

Illustrations by Dixie Burrus Browning

The University of North Carolina Press · Chapel Hill

North Carolina Parade

Stories
of History and People

Richard Walser
and
Julia Montgomery Street

Reprinted with permission

by

Broadfoot's of Wendell

6624 Robertson Pond Road
Wendell, North Carolina 27591

First printing, May 1966
Second printing, June 1979
Third printing, July 1991
Fourth printting, July 1998

Contents

Virginia Dare   3
North Carolina Indians   8
Blackbeard the Pirate   15
Susan Carter's Silk Dress   20
Wildlife in Early North Carolina   30
Lure of a Distant Land   37
A Palace and a War   45
The Hornet's Nest   50
Flora Macdonald   57
Hoecake for Breakfast   62
The State Capitol in Raleigh   69
The Golden Doorstop   73
The Boys' Anstalt at Salem   80
Cherokee Hero   88
Life of a Poet   97
Runaway Apprentice   102
Louisa and the State Song   107
Dr. Mitchell's Mountain   112

We Are Called "Tar Heels"   120
Dark Nights and High Tides   125
At Lucy Bennett's Farmhouse   132
"Thar She Blows"   138
Tobacco and Buck Duke   147
A Beauty and a Beast in the World of Wildflowers   153
Bread, Beauty, and Brotherhood   161
The Wright Brothers at Kitty Hawk   170
Captain Cat   176
Jugtown   184
Young Thomas Wolfe   190
The Research Triangle Park   194
Battleship   200
Old Christmas   205

North Carolina
Parade

VIRGINIA DARE

THE FIRST CHILD OF ENGLISH PARENTS TO BE BORN IN AMERICA was Virginia Dare, whose birth took place on Roanoke Island in North Carolina. How this came about is an interesting story.

Look at a map, and you will see that North Carolina is separated from the huge Atlantic Ocean by a series of narrow sandbanks, sometimes only wide enough for a few beach cottages and a highway. Between the sandbanks and the mainland, where the farms and towns are, you can see on the map many bodies of water called sounds. These sounds are dotted here and there with islands, most of them quite tiny. The largest one is Roanoke Island.

Ships move from the Atlantic Ocean to the sounds through breaks in the sandbanks called inlets. Many of these inlets are so shallow that only small boats can sail through them, and sometimes big ships strike bottom and often are wrecked.

Long ago, not quite a hundred years after the discovery of America by Columbus in 1492, North Carolina was inhabited entirely by Indians. At that time, the English people called all the land on the American coast by the name of Virginia. The name was in honor of the red-haired, unmarried Elizabeth I, Queen of England. Though sea captains and explorers claimed the land of Virginia for their queen, the Indians did not know this. They continued to think of the land as belonging only to them and their tribes.

Meanwhile, in far-away England, an adventurous friend of Queen Elizabeth, Sir Walter Raleigh, made plans to send a group of people to colonize America. He felt that Spain, England's enemy, might send settlers there and claim the land for their king. Then England would have to fight Spain to decide who owned Virginia. Queen Elizabeth told Sir Walter to go ahead and place a colony of English people in Virginia. But she would not let Sir Walter go with them. She wanted him to stay behind in England to advise her on the country's business.

So it was that Sir Walter Raleigh got together enough money to outfit a colony. The first colony of men was a failure. Shortly after arriving at Roanoke Island, they were in trouble with the Indians, who did not want the strange white men from England to claim their lands. The colonists did not feel very safe inside the fort they had built, and the men became lonesome because they had left their wives in England. When they ran out of food, they returned to England as soon as they could.

Sir Walter was disappointed, but he decided to try once more to put a colony in the New World. This time he would send women and children along with the men. Also, he would see that they had all the supplies they needed.

In 1587, two years after the failure of the first colony, a new group of people came to Roanoke Island. The little ships slipped through the inlet between the sandbanks near Roanoke Island and landed on July 22. They found the old fort and also the cottages that had been built by the first colonists; these they repaired and also built new ones.

A few days later, hostile Indians came to Roanoke Island and killed one of Governor John White's assistants. This frightened the settlers, for they were without any friends in the New World except for a gentle Indian named Manteo and his tribe of Croatans. Another Indian, Wanchese, was their bitter enemy.

In the midst of all these difficulties, Virginia Dare was born on Monday, August 18, 1587. Her father was Ananias Dare, another of Governor White's assistants, and her mother was Eleanor Dare, Governor White's own daughter. Thus the baby girl was granddaughter of the governor of the colony. Named Virginia because she was the first English child ever born in that part of the world, she was baptized the following Sunday.

The colonists were very happy with this new baby among them, but their troubles increased. Winter was coming on, and they were worried about supplies and food. They met together and urged Governor White to return to England to attend to these matters for them. At first he refused to leave his little settlement, but finally he gave in to their pleas and left for England on August 27.

When the governor reached England, his country was at war with Spain. It was not until three years later that Governor White was able to return to Roanoke Island. He found no one there. All the colonists, including the child Virginia Dare, had disappeared. What had happened to them? To this day we do not know. Perhaps they were captured by the Indians. Perhaps they went inland, looking for food, and were lost. At any rate, we now speak of Virginia Dare and the hundred men and women who disappeared with her as The Lost Colony.

Paul Green wrote a play about them, which he called *The Lost Colony*. This play has been given each summer at Roanoke Island on the exact spot where Governor White had his fort and where the unlucky settlement stood.

Though Virginia Dare vanished from history after only nine days of her life, legend has completed her story. We are told that Virginia Dare, under the protection of her friend Manteo, grew into a beautiful young woman. She was loved by a handsome Indian named O-kis-ko, but an evil magician, jealous of their happiness, turned her into a White Doe. O-kis-ko discovered that she would change back to her human form if her heart was pierced by an arrow made from oyster pearl.

One day the Indians went on a hunting trip to Roanoke Island, where the White Doe lived. With a silver arrow given him by Queen Elizabeth, the wicked Wanchese planned to slay the deer. During the hunt, the White Doe was seen dashing into the dark forest. Both O-kis-ko and Wanchese shot their arrows, and both the pearl arrow and the silver arrow entered the heart of the White Doe at the same moment. The deer changed back into the beautiful girl Virginia Dare, but she was dying. O-kis-ko was heartbroken.

Today, when we visit the old fort on Roanoke Island, it is said that we can see, on moonlit nights, a White Doe leaping into the shadowy pine trees nearby. It is Virginia Dare's spirit, which will never die.

NORTH CAROLINA INDIANS

IT IS BELIEVED THAT INDIANS LIVED IN NORTH CAROLINA FOR TEN to twenty thousand years before the white man reached her shores.

Archaeologists, who have uncovered evidence of the daily life of North Carolina's first inhabitants, say that the red men of ten thousand years ago were hunters. These nomadic hunters, following their food supplies, tracked down big game such as the mammoth, the giant ground sloth, the elk, the camel, the bison, and many varieties of smaller game, killing them with clubs and spears. Hunters lived in small family groups, constantly on the move, probably taking shelter in caves or hastily erected brush arbors wherever they made camp.

About five thousand years ago, the hunters began to make their camps near good sources of food supplies, the ocean and rivers, and to gather other forms of food such as berries, nuts, bark, and roots. They learned that they could grind these foods into a paste between two stones and mix them with meats to make more savory food. They also learned how to hollow out soft soapstone into bowls in which they could cook their food.

Although the hunters and gatherers still relied on the spear as their only weapon, they began to make better-balanced spears, which they could throw more accurately and effectively. They still traveled a great deal, but they gradually began to settle in villages. Here they grew corn, beans, and squash to supplement their diet of meat and wild vegetables; and they made clay pots to replace the stone utensils they had formerly used. Thus the hunters and gatherers became farmers.

These early farmers learned to make bows and arrows and to fashion sharper-pointed and slenderer spears that were much more effective weapons than their old cumbersome long spears with big stone points. The early farmers erected round houses of rushes and reeds, in place of the crude temporary shelters of their ancestors. For over a thousand years the early farmers lived, hunted, and grew crops throughout the Coastal Plain and the Piedmont. Finally they were driven off by invaders from the south.

The invaders, thought to have been a branch of the Creek Nation from Alabama and Georgia, made their homes in large stockaded villages near the rich fertile bottom lands of the Pee Dee River in the southern Piedmont area of the state. They built domed houses of poles, tied together at the top with ropes of fiber and covered with skins and bark. Their stockades were guarded by sentries, stationed in lookout towers, to ward off the natives whom they had driven away but who kept returning.

Corn was the most important crop grown by the in-

vaders, but squash, beans, and pumpkins were also culti-
vated by them, as well as tobacco for smoking and gourds
for making utensils and ceremonial masks and rattles.

The invaders were very religious people, who centered
all of their social, political, and religious activities around a
Ceremonial Center, erected on a high bluff on the Little
River near its meeting with Town Creek in Montgomery
County. This Center consisted of a large tract of land
enclosed by a row of logs set upright in the ground, protecting the Sacred Burial Mound and other structures. The
Center was also used in time of siege as a refuge. The invaders were a strong and resourceful people, but they were
not strong enough to hold their Piedmont home, and they
were driven out by the Siouan descendants of the very
tribes they themselves had forced away.

While the Piedmont Indians were largely Sioux, the
majority of Indians whom the early English colonists encountered in the coastal regions of North Carolina were of
Algonquin stock. These were the Croatans, the Hatteras,
the Chowan, the Weapomeiock, Corees, and other small,
weak tribes who were by turns friendly and hostile to the
white colonists.

After the failure of Sir Walter Raleigh's attempted
settlements (1585-87), the Carolina Indians encountered few
whites for nearly fifty years, until colonists from Virginia
began to trickle into the Albemarle region. The settlers
started making peace treaties with the Indians and trying
to buy up the land from them, but hostilities flared. The
white invaders prevailed, and the coastal Indians largely
disappeared or were absorbed into stronger confederations
such as the powerful and fierce Tuscaroras.

The Tuscaroras, who lived in the district between the Neuse and the Pamlico Rivers, were a branch of the Iroquois Nation. They were hunters, farmers, and traders. They traded their own products with more westerly tribes for furs, which in turn were traded to the settlers for guns, beads, pipes, axes, and rum. They were extremely fond of rum, and a Tuscarora would frequently drink up all he possessed before he reached home from a trading trip.

As white settlers began to move into the land claimed by the Tuscaroras, the latter became more and more hostile and finally began a war with the terrible massacre of September 22, 1711, at New Bern. This war, which lasted for three years, cost the lives of hundreds of white people and thousands of Indians, and it resulted in the ultimate defeat of the Tuscaroras. Those that were left of the once proud and numerous tribe eventually migrated to what is now New York state to join their Iroquois brethren. Thus the coastal and eastern sections of North Carolina were almost completely stripped of native inhabitants by the middle of the eighteenth century.

In the early 1700's the Piedmont was occupied by scattered villages of Indians who were known as the Eastern Sioux. In the Charlotte area and the Yadkin River valley dwelt the Catawbas; near Salisbury, the Saponi; around Asheboro, the Keyauwee; in the vicinity of Leaksville, the Saura; and in Orange County, the Occoneechee. An early traveler, surveyor, and historian, John Lawson, has told of these and other tribes in a fascinating book called *Lawson's History of North Carolina*.

The Catawbas were the most numerous and the most warlike of the Eastern Sioux and bitter enemies of the powerful Cherokee, whose mountain domain they frequently invaded with large war parties. They were, however, generally friendly to the English settlers, though they did join their enemies, the Cherokee, in 1715 to raid the settlements of the intruding white man.

The strong and numerous Cherokee, who controlled the whole mountain region of North Carolina as well as large areas in Virginia, Tennessee, South Carolina, Georgia, and Alabama, were farmers, hunters, and craftsmen. They grew quantities of tobacco as well as large crops of corn and many kinds of vegetables. They wove handsome baskets of river cane, honeysuckle vine, and oak splints, and they carved ceremonial masks from wood with efficient tools of bone and flint rock. Their weapons were bows and arrows, spears, and blowguns made of cane until they obtained their first guns about 1700. They were also excellent potters and fond of elaborate ornaments that they constructed from bone, stone, and copper and traded to other tribes to the north.

The Cherokee probably saw his first white man in 1540 when DeSoto, the Spaniard from Florida, made a trip into the North Carolina mountains in search of gold. From that time until well into the nineteenth century, the history of relations between the Cherokee and the paleface was one of peace and war, peace and war.

The most famous Indian in the story of North America was a half-Cherokee called Sequoya, who, alone and uneducated, invented an entire Cherokee alphabet, resulting in the first written native American language. This was a feat accomplished by no other man in the history of the world. This alphabet was so practical that the formerly uneducated

Cherokee were able to read and write their own tongue within a short time. Soon they attained a high degree of civilization, building houses like the white man's, using spinning wheels and looms, and keeping cows and cats. No other tribes had done any of these things before.

Civilization and education did not solve the Cherokee's ever-growing problem of holding their lands against the invading white man. The more the settlers moved westward in the state, the more the Cherokee were forced from their ancestral lands, and the farther into the mountains they were forced to retreat. Finally, in a bitterly fought battle of words, the Congress of the United States, urged on by President Andrew Jackson, voted to remove all Cherokee across the Mississippi River and resettle them in Indian Territory (now the state of Oklahoma).

This removal of a whole nation, one of the darkest blots on the records of the United States government, is often referred to as "The Trail of Tears" because of the hardships the Indians suffered on the journey, prodded along by brutal soldiers and plagued by hunger, cold, and sickness. Thousands of Cherokee died along the way. Only a few of the Indians, who hid out in the Smoky Mountains, escaped this terrible trek. It is the descendants of these brave people who now make up the eastern band of Cherokee. They dwell on a reservation known as the Qualla Boundary, in the heart of the Great Smokies, with the town of Cherokee as their Center.

Once North Carolina was wholly peopled by the red man, but now the only material evidence of his existence within her borders consists of several hundred Cherokee in the western part of the state, the even fewer Lumbees or

Croatans in Richmond and Robeson Counties, an occasional arrowhead or other Indian artifact turned up by a plow or an observant collector, and the results of excavations and reconstructions of archaeologists.

With the help of the State Department of Archives and History, archaeologists have unearthed the site and reconstructed a village of the invaders, Town Creek Indian Mound near Mt. Gilead in Montgomery County. This is open most of the time for the benefit of the public.

In the western part of the state, there has been constructed a Cherokee Indian Village called Oconaluftee, near the site of the outdoor drama, *Unto These Hills*. This village and the drama present an authentic picture of several phases of Indian life. Unfortunately, the Cherokee Museum, which was a priceless treasure house of the tribe's history, burned in 1963.

Other museums in the state, including the State Museum in Raleigh, the Old Salem Museum in Winston-Salem, as well as many private collections, contain extensive and enlightening exhibits of North Carolina Indian life.

BLACKBEARD THE PIRATE

AT FIRST, THE COLONIES THAT ENGLAND SET UP ON THE ATLANTIC coastline were very weak. They had few soldiers and sailors to protect them. An evil pirate like Blackbeard could steal and kill when he wanted to. Nobody, not even the Governor of North Carolina, was strong enough to stop him. There were many pirates along the North Carolina coast. But Blackbeard was the meanest.

He was born in England and, when only a boy, left home to go to sea as a sailor. He noticed how weak the colonies were and decided to become a member of a pirate crew. So fearless and bold was he that soon he was the captain of his own ship, the *Queen Anne's Revenge.*

He fought ships at sea, killed their crews, and stole their cargoes. When afraid he would be caught, he slipped away to the North Carolina coast. He did this because the North Carolina coast had many coves and sounds behind the sand bars where he could hide. North Carolina became his headquarters. By now, no one remembered his real name. The name Blackbeard was enough to make people shake with terror, and he liked this.

Blackbeard was a tall, strong man—fearful to look at. He would take locks of his long black hair and beard, twist them into little pigtails, and bind them with colored ribbons. During a battle with an unfortunate ship, he would tie slow-burning matches to the pigtails near his forehead. He looked as if he might explode any minute, like a firecracker. Hanging from his shoulders down across his chest was a leather belt with six pistols, all cocked and ready to shoot. He carried a sword in his strong hand.

Most pirate captains attacked only weak vessels, but not Blackbeard. He was so brazen that he went after warships too. He was not afraid of anybody. Once he took his fleet to Charlestown, South Carolina, and took over the town. The Governor of South Carolina and his officials looked on helplessly.

Early in 1718, Blackbeard heard that the King of England would pardon all pirates who turned themselves in. Blackbeard sailed up to see Governor Charles Eden of North Carolina and surrendered himself and twenty of his men. It was reported that Governor Eden was a friend of Blackbeard, because he gave the Governor part of his booty. We do not know whether this is true or not but certainly Governor Eden was easy on pirates.

For a while, Blackbeard stopped being a pirate. He bought a big house in North Carolina, gave fine parties, and made a great display of the money and jewels he had stolen. He married a girl sixteen years old and Governor Eden performed the ceremony. The poor girl did not know she was wife number fourteen, with twelve still living in other parts of the world.

After a while, this kind of life began to bore Blackbeard, and he decided to go back to pirating. He went to sea and captured so many ships that the Governor of Virginia asked Governor Eden to stop him. But Governor Eden had no intention of curbing this evil man.

Finally, the Governor of Virginia would put up with Blackbeard no longer. He asked Lieutenant Robert Maynard to go out and take Blackbeard, dead or alive. Lieutenant Maynard sailed with two small sloops for Ocracoke Island off the North Carolina coast, where he knew Blackbeard was hiding.

Several days later, at sundown, he saw Blackbeard's ship, *Adventure,* anchored off Ocracoke. The pirate was not surprised to see the sloops, for Governor Eden's secretary had written him a letter to warn him. But he was not worried. While Maynard was busy all night getting ready to fight, Blackbeard spent the night drinking.

At sunrise on November 22, 1718, Lieutenant Maynard began the fight. First, he sent out rowboats and the smaller sloop. The rowboats retreated when Blackbeard fired upon them, and the sloop stuck on a sand bar. Maynard's sloop, the *Ranger,* now had to attack alone.

Blackbeard shouted out when the *Ranger* was near, "You villains! Where do you come from?"

At this, Maynard ordered the British flag run up on the mast. He yelled back, "You can see by our colors that we are not pirates."

"Send over a boat so that I can see you," replied Blackbeard.

"I cannot spare my boat," said Maynard, "but I will come aboard your ship from my sloop as soon as I can."

Blackbeard ran up his flag, the skull and crossbones, and fired at the *Ranger*. Since Lieutenant Maynard's sloop had no heavy guns, he ordered his men to lie still on the deck or to go below. When the smoke cleared, Blackbeard saw few men, and he thought he had killed most of the sailors. The *Ranger* drifted closer to Blackbeard's *Adventure*. Finally, the two ships touched. Blackbeard cried out to his men, "Jump on board and cut to pieces those that are alive."

As the pirates boarded the *Ranger,* Maynard's men came to life. Blackbeard could not believe his eyes, but he ordered his men to fight with everything they had. There was a terrible struggle. There were shouts, pistol shots, and groans.

Suddenly, Blackbeard and Maynard stood face to face. They fired at each other. Blackbeard missed, and Maynard's bullet went right through the pirate, but the tough man went on fighting. Each drew his sword, and Blackbeard swung at Maynard and injured him. One of Maynard's men wounded the pirate in the throat, but still Blackbeard fought on. Then, as he was loading a pistol, Blackbeard fell dead.

The pirate crew quickly surrendered. The fight was over.

Later, Maynard counted twenty-five wounds in Blackbeard's body, five of them from pistol shots. Maynard then took his sword and, with a great sweep, cut Blackbeard's head from his body. He tied the awful-looking thing to the bowsprit of the *Ranger* and sailed away.

The days of the cruel pirates were ended.

Today, the island of Ocracoke is calm and peaceful. Many people take their vacations there. The beautiful blue waters off Ocracoke tell nothing of the terrible last day of Blackbeard.

SUSAN CARTER'S
SILK DRESS

MISTRESS CARTER SWISHED INTO THE HIGH-CEILINGED, ORNATELY furnished drawing room, her skirts rustling with a silky whisper.

"Oh, Mother, you have another new silk dress!" exclaimed Susan, jumping up from the sofa where she was dangling a string for a white kitten to catch.

"Isn't it pretty?" Mrs. Carter twirled around, showing off the puffs of the rose-sprigged satin overskirt over the full, blue dress. "Mistress Smith just finished it in time for my tea party."

Susan touched the shimmering fabric with an exploratory finger. "It's just beautiful, Mother. I'm sure it is the prettiest gown in Brunswick Town. The color is just like the sky, and you've used your new lace from France for the sleeve and bodice ruffles."

"My, what a time I had, getting this shade of blue dye," Mrs. Carter said. She was now arranging the tea table that a slave girl had just laid with snowy linen, silver, and flowered china. "I must have tried a dozen lots of indigo to get the proper hue."

Susan sighed and waggled the string for the kitten. "I wish I could have a silk dress, Mother. One just like yours."

"You shall have one, Susan, when you are thirteen."

"Thirteen? That's months away. I haven't been twelve very long."

"Time flies quickly, my dear, especially when you're busy, and you will be very busy, soon." Mrs. Carter tripped to the door to greet her guests before Susan could ask what she meant.

The entering ladies, perfumed and powdered, were all dressed in beautiful silken, lace-trimmed gowns that rippled and rustled as they walked daintily across the flowered carpet. Susan spread her pink calico skirt with one hand and curtsied to Mistress Dobbs, wife of the Royal Governor of Carolina. She curtsied to Mistress Harnett and turned toward Mistress Hepburn, when a shrill whistle sounded through the open windows.

Susan fled, dropping the kitten to follow the trailing string. "I'm coming, James!" she called to her red-headed brother as she sped across the broad portico and leaped to the ground, ignoring the steps. "Is the merchantman coming in? Whew! I almost got caught in Mother's tea party. You should have seen the beautiful gowns, James. All the

ladies are elegantly dressed, and Mother's new sky-blue silk
is the prettiest dress of them all. I shall have one just like
it next year."

"Oh, you and your silk dress," James was scornful. "All
you think about is that dress you'll have some day. When
you get a silk dress you'll be no more good to play with.
You'll be just like all the other girls in town. Prissy."

"I will not!" Susan's blue eyes blazed, and she shook her
blonde curls. "I will not. Besides, I'll wear it only to balls
and parties."

"Balls! Parties! Pft!" James kicked at a beetle hurrying across the gravel path, and handed Susan the big, red
apple he was crunching.

She bit a mouthful from the fresh side. "Well, a girl
can't be a tomboy forever. Mother says so." Susan giggled.
"Come on, let's run. I hear the bell clanging at the
port."

They ran hand in hand down the live-oak-shaded street
that led to the docks of Brunswick Town on the Cape Fear
River, the largest port in the province of North Carolina.

Susan shaded her eyes with a freckled hand. "Oh, look
at her, James, sailing up the river like a big, white bird.
Isn't she a beauty? It *is* Father's *Merchant Queen*. I can't
wait to see what she brought for my special present this
time."

"Thank goodness she didn't meet pirates," James said.
"Father said she would be loaded with a cargo from France.
It's a good thing Mother is occupied with her party this
afternoon, or she'd never allow you on the docks to watch
the unloading."

The two raced on. "I wonder what Father had sent for

me this time," Susan panted. "I know it will be something fine."

"I'm getting a gun," James bragged. "A real, steel-barrel, silver-mounted gun from France, for my very own."

"Humph! Who wants an old gun," Susan sniffed, as they stopped at their father's berths on the wharf.

The captain was just climbing to the pier from the *Merchant Queen's* small boat. "Good day to you, Mistress Susan, Master James." He bowed low and kissed the hand Susan held out.

"What did Father have you bring me this time, Captain Moore?" Susan could not take time to be polite. "What is it? I'm dying of curiosity."

"You'll be fair surprised, little lady," Captain Moore replied. "It's something very special. Something I hear you've been longing for."

"A silk gown," Susan guessed, and the captain smiled knowingly but did not answer except to say, "Excuse me. I must see to my passengers. They do not speak a word of English." He turned and said something in French to a bewildered-looking man and woman standing apart, with a frightened-looking girl clinging to the woman's hand. All three were dressed very plainly in heavy, dark woolen clothing and wooden sabots.

"The Frenchmen," Captain Moore said to Susan and James, who had followed him to meet the strangers. "They've come to Brunswick Town to instruct your father's people in the art of sericulture, that is, the raising of silkworms and the spinning and weaving of silk."

"Silkworms?" asked Susan. "Does silk come from

worms? Real, sure-enough creepy, crawly, wiggly worms? Mother gets her silk from abroad. It's cloth."

"Silk cloth is woven from thread," the captain informed her, "and silk thread comes from worms, silkworms."

"Didn't you know that, stupid?" James put in. "Lots of people in the Provinces raise silkworms, but we've never had any here."

"You'll have them from now on," Captain Moore said. "Hadn't you heard that Governor Dobbs is requiring every plantation owner to plant at least ten mulberry trees and raise silkworms?"

"Father has acres of mulberry trees on Carter Plantation upriver," Susan said. "Is that what silkworms eat? Mulberries?"

"Mulberry leaves, dimwit," commented James, disgusted at his ignorant sister. "Everybody knows that."

"Where'll we get the silkworms?" Susan asked.

"That's where your present comes in, Mistress Susan," the captain replied. "Right here, in my pocket, I have a cane full of silkworm eggs from the finest strain in France. They are for you. The others are stored on the *Merchant Queen*."

"Worms!" Susan seemed dumfounded. "Father got me worms for a present? He wouldn't play a trick on me like that!" She turned her back so no one would see her tears; then she flung up her head proudly and laughed. "Worms! Silkworms! What an interesting and unusual present. Father is always so original."

"Father means for you to raise your own silk dress," James mocked and ran off to wait for his new gun to be unloaded.

Susan noticed that the French girl was trying hard not to give way to her fright in these strange surroundings, and she momentarily forgot her own disappointment to comfort her.

"My name is Susan," she said, in a warm friendly voice, and pointed to herself. "What is yours?"

The girl understood at once and replied, "Celeste."

"Welcome to Brunswick Town, Celeste," Susan said. "I hope you will like our fair land of Carolina. Come on home with me."

Celeste blinked and murmured a question in French.

The captain translated the speeches. "Celeste says she will be happy to go home with you, Susan. You are kind to make her feel welcome."

"I hope you will help me grow a silk dress," Susan added.

At the word *silk,* Celeste brightened up, and she eagerly accompanied Susan, her wooden sabots clacking on the cobbles as they crossed the street and entered the yard of Squire Carter's beautiful mansion.

The French family was established in a snug house on Carter Plantation, where they set about to begin the culture of silk. From that very first day, Susan and Celeste became fast friends and were soon able to chatter to each other in a mixture of languages that each could understand. Susan spent much of her time at the plantation, to the disappointment of James, who finally gave in to the idea that she would not remain his tomboy playmate forever. Her "present" of silkworm eggs seemed to absorb all of her time.

Celeste showed Susan how the eggs, which had been kept cold all winter, must be placed just so on large, flat boards to hatch in the warm sun. From then on, their excitement in "growing a dress" grew with the fast-maturing, tiny, white, thread-like worms that emerged from the pinhead-sized eggs. They gathered mulberry leaves frantically and chopped them up to feed the squirming creatures that seemed to eat greedily all of the time.

When the worms had grown to twice their size, they were moved to larger flats, where they ate and ate and ate, until Susan and Celeste thought they could not possibly keep enough mulberry leaves gathered to feed them. The large shed, where Susan's eggs were kept in a corner to themselves, was constantly a-hum with the grinding, crunching sound made by the thousands and thousands of wriggling creatures that chewed noisily on the ever-increasing number of leaves they must be fed each day. As the worms approached their maximum size of three inches, everybody on the plantation, the slaves from the mansion, and even James who grumbled constantly, worked from morning until night to feed the gluttons.

At the end of six weeks, the worms suddenly stopped eating and began rearing their heads and waving them about. Susan thought it the funniest sight she had ever seen. Now it was time to start placing the silkworms, one by one, on branches of trees and brush, stuck upright in boxes of sand. These were the supports for the cocoons that the worms would spin.

"Ugh!" Susan repeated over and over. "This is the hardest, dirtiest work I've ever done. I feel that I'll scream if I have to touch one more worm."

"Think of your silk dress," Celeste would remind her, and Susan kept doggedly on.

The five days the silkworms took to spin their cocoons flew by, while Susan and Celeste lounged and slept at the mansion, planning and dreaming. At least, Susan dreamed and talked, and Celeste listened wistfully to her schemes for having the wonderful silk dyed, cut, and sewed into the most gorgeous gown a girl ever had.

"First, *ma chère*," Celeste said, "*Maman* must weave the thread into cloth."

"I'm glad your mamma is a weaver," Susan replied. "If I had to wait for the thread to be sent to France or England to be woven, then back here to be dyed and made, I'd be fifteen years old before I ever got my dress, instead of thirteen. It's a good thing Father is having looms made."

"Of course, Suzanne. That's why we came to this wild land. *Maman* and *Papa* have been silk raisers and weavers all their lives. Your father offered them much money to come here and teach their art to the people, so the thread wouldn't have to be sent to France. Oh, beautiful France! How happy I will be to see her again!"

"You mean you want to leave Carolina?" Susan asked in disbelief.

"France is our home, Suzanne. This is a savage country. Only yesterday, I saw a red Indian skulking about. I fear them."

Susan laughed merrily. "You needn't be afraid of the Indians around here, Celeste. They are all friendly. Why, it's been years since there's been a scalping."

Celeste clapped her hands over her dark hair and said no more.

When the five days were over, everyone at the mansion piled into carriages and wagons to join the plantation people in gathering the cocoons. They worked like machines trying to get the cocoons to the steam vats where the larvae would be killed before they should pierce the ends of the envelopes and ruin the thread. They saved many of the largest and best cocoons so the moths could hatch and lay eggs for next year.

After the steaming, they worked just as hard spreading the cream-colored balls in the sun to dry. Then these were stored in big baskets with holed lids from which the reelers would draw out the silk. Susan's excitement grew as she helped with the tiring work.

Finally, the big day came, and the very first silken threads that were reeled on Squire Carter's plantation were those from Susan's special present. She could not take her eyes off Celeste's father as he twirled the handle of the reel with one hand, and with the other fed onto it five strands like cobwebs, so fine they were almost invisible, from the five holes in the lid of the cocoon basket. She was prouder than any queen, when he finally handed her a great reel of genuine silk thread.

"Now," Susan rejoiced to Celeste, "we will get your mama to weave this into raw silk cloth. Then my mama will see to having it dyed and cut and sewed into two beautiful silk gowns. Oh, Celeste! Isn't it marvelous?"

"Two silk dresses?" Celeste questioned in surprise. "Ah, but are you not satisfied with one dress?"

"Two." Susan's eyes sparkled, and she flipped her blond curls. "One for me, and one for you. Just think of it, Celeste. We've grown our very own silk dresses!"

"Yah!" jeered James, who had crept behind them to eavesdrop. "Silk dresses! Humph! A gun is a thousand times better." But he joined in their laughter as they ran off to show the wonderful thread to Susan's mother.

Like the cultivation of indigo and of rice, sericulture and silk cloth manufacture never grew to be a large industry in North Carolina, but it was an important one for well over two hundred years. Eastern North Carolina was a natural habitat of the white mulberry tree, and its climate was perfect for nurturing silkworms. The quality of the raw silk produced was excellent, and the profits from the operation enormous. But the work required was tremendous, and even the abundance of slave labor before 1865 was not enough to keep the home-manufactories going.

From 1731 to 1755, 40,756 pounds of raw silk were exported from North and South Carolina, but by the time artificial silk was introduced to the world in 1889, the amount had dwindled to a mere trickle.

Textile manufacturing is now the largest industry in North Carolina, with cotton and synthetics—rayon, nylon, dacron, and other polyfibers—being processed in more mills and by more workers than in any other state in the union. Real silk, however, is no longer grown, and very little of it is processed in the Old North State.

WILDLIFE
IN EARLY NORTH CAROLINA

BEFORE THE WHITE MAN CAME TO NORTH CAROLINA, THE INDIANS were surrounded by an abundance of everything they required for a comfortable and happy existence. The coastal waters and the rivers were crowded with fish, the fields and forests were alive with all manner of game and fowl, the climate was temperate, and the soil fertile. The red man knew no game laws, but he practiced natural conservation by killing only what he needed for food, clothing, and protection, leaving the bulk of the wildlife to maintain its natural balance.

On the Coastal Plain, the Chowan Indian drew his bow and shot a bone-tipped arrow, feathered with paroquet plumage, straight to the heart of the great cat that had screamed outside his lodge in the night. He had finally come upon it crouching in a tree, ready to spring on the white-tail deer that grazed among the live-oaks. The chase had been long and dangerous, but the Chowanook was hardy and unafraid. His cunning was equal to that of the panther itself, and his stout weapon could bring down any large animal he met—deer, bear, wolf, or panther. His wife would serve venison stew or bear meat for the evening meal, and when winter came, his children would keep warm beneath the tawny-gold pelt of the animal.

At the same time, perhaps, a Catawba warrior sped on silent feet across a green meadow in the wide Yadkin Valley of the Piedmont, his stone-tipped spear held high. With a mighty thrust he plunged it deep into the soft flesh behind the left front leg of the shaggy, humped beast on the edge of a herd at the riverside. That evening his squaw would serve him buffalo tongue, and they would delight in the possession of another thick, warm skin to make soft the bed of their children.

In the mountains, westward, a Cherokee brave left his field of ripening corn to go after the Great Wapiti (elk) that his young son had reported seeing among the big trees beyond the lodges and fields. As the hunter crept noiselessly through the undergrowth and reached the rim of the forest, he spotted the majestic creature, raising its antlered head to nibble at the leaves of a poplar. He brought down the animal with a flint-barbed arrow, shot from a bow as tall as himself. An elk was a rare prize that would feed a whole village and make a set of garments suitable for the hunter who brought one in.

In every section of North Carolina big and lesser game was plentiful for the Indians' taking.

When Captains Philip Amadas and Arthur Barlowe,

scouting the New World for Sir Walter Raleigh in 1584, landed on Roanoke Island, Amadas wrote for his patron:

"This island has many goodly woods, full of deer, conies, hares and fowl, even in the midst of summer, in incredible abundance." And he added, "Such a flock of cranes (for the most part white) arose under us with a cry . . . as if an army of men had shouted together."

A year later, Thomas Hariot, who was with the first hundred men attempting to colonize that island, wrote of the abundance of fish in the ocean and the sounds. He described the Indian's methods of catching fish in a weir (a fence made of stakes set in the water) and cooking or drying them on sticks set around fires. He, too, marveled at the amount of game and wildfowl to be taken.

After the failure of the English attempts at colonization in the latter 1500's, supposedly because of starvation in part, the wildlife in North Carolina remained stable for half a century or so. But when settlers from Virginia began to trickle into the Albemarle region in the second quarter of the 1600's, they marked the beginning of the end of the enormous bounty of forest, field, and stream. With traps and guns they hunted the fur-bearers and shipped pelts by the thousands to Europe, where furs were in great demand. With hook, line, and seine they over-fished the rivers, and they destroyed the beavers' dams and otters' runs. As the country became more and more settled, the balance of wildlife became more and more unbalanced. The colonists, like the Indians, practiced no game laws, but unlike their red countrymen, they killed wantonly and recklessly, giving no thought to conservation.

John Lawson, North Carolina's first historian, who traveled through the colony from Charlestown in 1701, wrote at length of the many and varied animals, birds, and "insects" he had not seen or heard of anywhere else in his thousand-mile journey. He described the buffalo or wild beef, the elk, wolf, panther, bear, deer, and a host of lesser creatures such as the possum, raccoon, otter, polecat, rabbit, squirrel, fox, and rat. All of these he said he saw with his own eyes, but admitted that he had not actually encountered a tiger, lion, or jackal, though told that they lived in Carolina.

Lawson listed and described a large number of songbirds and game birds of the interior and the coast, including the great bald eagle and the wild turkey. As "insects" he noted alligators, land and water tortoises, scorpion-lizards, frogs of many kinds, land and water terrapins, and a wide variety of reptiles, both poisonous and harmless.

John Lawson's *History of North Carolina* was first published in England in 1709, with other editions in 1714, 1718, and 1722. A poorly done volume appeared in North Carolina in 1860, and an edited version, with plates and maps, was printed in Virginia in 1952.

Throughout the 1700's, writers frequently mentioned game animals and birds but gave little space to fish. Baron Von Graffenried, founder of New Bern and companion of John Lawson's last and fatal journey among the Tuscaroras, recorded seeing buffalo in 1728. Bishop Spangenberg, traveling through the colony in 1751 seeking a proper site for a Moravian settlement, mentioned finding buffalo tracks and trails near the Catawba River in the Brushy Mountains.

The Moravians, who settled in the present Forsyth

County in 1753, were much concerned with the wolves and panthers that disturbed their colony. One of the first entries in the diary of the thirteen brethren who made up an advance group records, "While we held Lovefeast the wolves howled loudly," and another the same year, "The wolves and panthers made themselves heard." As late as 1775 the diarist of the village of Bethabara wrote under the date of July 18, "The wolves came into the orchard last night, and killed and ate two lambs and one grown sheep." Although the Moravian Brethren killed many bear, deer, and small game for food and for the hides, which were valuable in commerce, they took only what they needed.

The diaries of the Moravian brethren contain many references to the enormous flocks of wild pigeons that at times darkened the sky as they flew over the Piedmont. As an example, on November 2, 1760, "Neighbors found the roosting place of the wild pigeons of which there are remarkably many. Next week some of the Brethren went to the same place and brought in 1800." And they record, "In the mornings the pigeons go off in clouds, at sunset returning to their camp, crowding so closely together that branches are broken off, and trees that have withstood many a heavy storm fall to the ground."

The mighty elk, largest of the eastern deer family, which once roamed the mountains and the Piedmont, was seldom seen in North Carolina after the end of the 1700's, and the buffalo deserted the area at about the same period. Wolves lingered in the Coastal Plain section and in the central part of the state until the late 1800's and in the mountains until the early 1900's. The last positive recording of a panther, an animal once plentiful over the whole of North Carolina, came from the coastal region in the first decade of this century, while the last known specimen of the Carolina wild pigeon succumbed in a zoo in 1904. The brilliant little native Carolina paroquet seems to have vanished also. The last two and a half centuries have seen the complete extinction of some animals and birds that were a part of early North Carolina.

When the Indians predicted that the invading white man would become "as numerous as the leaves of the trees," they also foresaw the disappearance of the abundant game so necessary for their own survival. Their predictions were correct.

Although North Carolina is still well supplied with bear, deer, small game, fish, and birds, including a few bald eagles and wild turkeys and what John Lawson termed "insects," the supply will not last forever. Unless careful conservation of all wildife is practiced and laws for the regulation of hunting and fishing are enforced, those species still living in the state will go the way of those that have been exterminated.

In the North Carolina Museum of Natural History in Raleigh, there can be seen some live and many mounted specimens of the wildlife native to the state now and in years gone by. In several towns and cities, Nature-Science Centers have been set up for the education of young people and adults interested in all phases of wildlife.

Near Asheville is the Blue Ridge Craggy Gardens Visitors' Center; in Burlington, The McDade Wildlife Museum; in Charlotte, The Children's Nature Museum; in Greensboro, The Greensboro Junior Museum; and in Rocky

36 North Carolina Parade

Mount, The Children's Museum. In Winston-Salem, The Nature-Science Center conducts classes in all branches of nature and wildlife and is collecting a fine library for the use of the public.

LURE
OF A DISTANT LAND

ONE BRIGHT, MELLOW INDIAN SUMMER DAY IN 1751, A BOY OF
sixteen strode through a forest trail in Piedmont North
Carolina, ahead of a small cavalcade. His keen blue eyes
watched for game, and his ears were alert for any unusual
sound. He was dressed in worn buckskins and moccasins,
with an old felt hat perched jauntily atop his black head
and a rifle as long as he was tall across a muscular right
shoulder. Behind him rode his father on horseback, and
his mother, sisters, and the smaller children followed in a
big covered wagon. A cart, loaded with looms, tools, and a
forge, rumbled behind the wagon; and cattle, swine, and
extra horses that were driven by two brothers brought up
the rear of the troop. Squire Boone and his wife, Sarah,

with most of their eleven children were nearing the end of a long, leisurely journey, during which their fourth son, Daniel, had been the more than willing scout and hunter.

Daniel was well fitted for the task because he had inherited a double portion of courage and daring from both of his parents, descendants of fearless Devonshire adventurers. He had grown up in William Penn's woods with friendly, peaceful Delaware Indians who were playmates and taught him woodcraft. Always a bold planner and dreamer, afraid of nothing, he was already on the way to becoming the mighty hunter and explorer who later opened up the path to the west for the white man, the famous Wilderness Road.

When he was just a young boy, Daniel had learned to track small game, fearlessly stalking rabbits, squirrels, and chipmunks in the dark forests around his Pennsylvania home. He could bring them down with a weapon of his own invention. This original killer was a short club with knotty roots on one end, and he had taught himself to throw it with deadly accuracy. As he grew, his skill as a woodsman and hunter had increased, and when he was twelve years old, his father had given him a rifle of his very own. That long rifle, taller then than the boy himself, was Daniel's pride and delight. It was such a wonderful possession that he, as was the custom, gave it a special name. He called the gun "Tick-licker," from the sound it made when he cocked it. For many a year "Tick-licker" proved a faithful companion, often saving Daniel from death, as well as providing him and his family with food.

The Boones were staunch, sturdy farmers, weavers, and blacksmiths, but they were restless folk, too, who could not bear to be crowded by close neighbors. When their section of Pennsylvania began to acquire more settlers and to develop a shortage of game, Squire Boone decided to look for a place where he could have plenty of "elbow room" and good hunting. He heard that the central part of North Carolina was just such a place, so he sold his farm near Oley, and the family started southward.

They did not hurry. They found the Shenandoah country through which they went so beautiful, and the traveling so pleasant, that they lingered along the way for more than a year, camping, grazing their livestock, and hunting. It had been a balmy spring day in 1750 when the Boones set out, and now in the autumn of 1751, Daniel and his father emerged from the forest on the top of a ridge to see, spread below them, an unbelievably beautiful valley. It was carpeted with broad meadows just waiting to be farmed, bordered by fine forests that must be full of game, and watered by a gently flowing river.

Squire Boone stood beside his son, looking at the rich prospect. "We have come home, Dan'l!" he exclaimed. "I heard tell that this Yadkin River Valley is the garden spot of the land. It's the truth. Just look at it, son. Did you ever see a prettier or more fruitful-looking land?"

"I never did, Pa," Daniel replied. "Why, I'll bet them woods is busting full of game. Like as not a fellow only needs to step amongst the trees down there to sight deer, bears, wildcats, panthers, whatever he's looking for."

"And all his, just for the hunting, Dan'l. There's not a settler in sight, either. Tomorrow I'll find the nearest town and see to buying up a place, while you and the boys start building a shelter for your ma and the least ones."

"Yes, sir, Pa," Daniel answered, leaning on the rifle. "I'll bet the game here is thicker'n fleas on a dog's back. Hist!" He raised an arm to silence his father and pointed. "Look! A bear down there in the broom-sedge." Daniel raised "Tick-licker" to his shoulder as if it were light as a feather and fired, then he let out a whoop that brought the whole family running.

"Whew! We'll have bear stew for supper tonight, sure as shooting," cried one of the younger boys. "Ma, can I help skin the critter? Can I have the claws to string for a neck-chain?"

"Ask Dan'l," Sarah Boone answered. "He killed the bear."

"Sure you can, Bud." Daniel roughed up the red hair of his little brother. "And Jenny can have the claws of the next one. Shucks! 'Twon't be any time till everybody in the Boone family will be wearing neck-chains of North Caroliny bear claws."

"No call to brag, Dan'l," Squire said. "That might have been just a piece of good luck. Now, let's us menfolks make camp, while your ma and the girls cook us up some supper."

Before many days had passed, the Boone family had raised a snug log cabin on the banks of the Yadkin River, not far from the traders' ford. This was a crossing on the Great Trading Path from Virginia to Georgia, along which trappers and traders drove their horses with loads of skins or trade goods. The Indians also used it to go from place to place.

Though Daniel had been happy enough in Pennsylvania tracking game, herding his father's cattle, playing with Indian companions and learning every phase of forest life, he was even happier here in the wilderness of the Yadkin Valley. From dawn to dark, sometimes for days, he wandered alone in the forest, looking and learning. His father sometimes urged him to take a turn at the loom or forge, or lend a hand in the fields, but finally stopped trying to coax him into domestic work. Squire gave him the joyous task of furnishing the table with meat and the women with animal skins for making clothing and coverings. Daniel never avoided this delightful duty but kept his mother and sisters more than well supplied. Each time he hunted, he roved farther and farther, as though called by the country that lay beyond the westward mountains.

By 1755 Squire Boone had moved to another location in the same fertile Yadkin Valley (a spot in the present Davie County) and settled there permanently.

From this home in the same year, Daniel went to war against the French and Indians, under General Braddock, as a wagoner and blacksmith. During the campaign, Daniel Boone met George Washington and, more important to him, a trader named John Finley. Finley had actually visited that land beyond the western North Carolina mountains which Daniel had so often wondered about. On the long daily marches and around the nightly campfires, John Finley told tales of the marvelous land of Caintuck (Kentucky) where no Indian tribes lived but where Shawnees, Cherokee, and others fought bloody battles or hunted game. There a man could just stand still and shoot buffalo, deer, and bears by the thousands, provided he could keep his scalp, John Finley declared. These stories fired Daniel Boone with a burning desire to go to Caintuck and set him to dreaming of settling in that hunter's paradise. Right then he resolved that some day he would go, no matter what came.

With Braddock's defeat, Daniel cut his wagon horse loose and galloped the long, weary miles back to his home on the Yadkin and took up his old life of hunting and farming with his parents. Three years later he married a black-eyed lass by the name of Rebecca Bryan. For the time being he had to lay aside his dream of exploring the land of Caintuck to attend his home and family, but he did not forget the dream. He had everything a man required—a good gun, a good horse, and a good wife—but Daniel Boone wanted more.

He and Rebecca lived for a time near his father, moved to Virginia for two years to escape the raiding Cherokee, then returned to North Carolina to settle farther west, in Wilkes County near the village that is now Ferguson. They built two homes, one on each side of the river, before they were satisfied. At least Rebecca seemed satisfied, but not Daniel. Kentucky kept calling him, and he kept on hunting and exploring farther and farther west, searching for a passage through the mountains to his dream.

It was on one of these trips through the Blue Ridge that Daniel Boone carved that famous legend on a beech tree in the edge of Tennessee:

> "D. Boon cilled a bar on this tree in
> the year 1760."

He may not have known how to spell, but there never lived a man better educated for life and survival in his time and situation.

During those wandering years of his young manhood,

Daniel did not fail to keep on adding to his knowledge of the ways of Indians and of animals. He knew the wilds so well that his acquaintances often said, "Daniel Boone thinks more like an Indian than an Indian himself," and, "Daniel Boone knows more about the ways of the wild than the game that lives there." It was valuable knowledge and paid enormous dividends for him and those who came after him.

The Cherokee, on the whole, were fairly peaceful most of the time, but as larger numbers of white settlers pushed them farther west, they grew more hostile and began to make raids on outlying cabins and farms. Daniel Boone recognized the seriousness of these forays, and he took up his gun with a will, becoming known as one of the greatest Indian fighters on the frontier. In spite of fighting them, Boone never showed hatred for the red man. Even when his oldest son was scalped and murdered and, in later years, when he himself was captured and tortured, he respected the Indian as a man.

On one occasion, while he still lived in the Piedmont, a Cherokee called Saucy Jack had several shooting matches with Daniel, but always lost to Boone's superior marksmanship. When Saucy Jack got angry and threatened to kill his opponent, Squire Boone went after him with a hatchet. Jack disappeared, never to be seen again, but he had taught Daniel a valuable lesson—never to allow himself to outshoot an Indian in a contest. By remembering this lesson and by his absolute fearlessness, Daniel saved his own life and many other lives in the years when the Cherokee and the Shawnee went on the warpath against the increasing numbers of white settlers.

On the first day of May, 1769, from his cabin in Wilkes County, Daniel Boone, with several companions, started out on his long-dreamed-of great adventure. John Finley had come knocking on his door after fourteen years of silence and interested him again in going to Kentucky. Finley guided the party. With "Tick-licker" over his shoulder, his old black felt hat at its accustomed rakish angle, and his buckskins swishing as he strode along, Daniel Boone set his blue eyes firmly on the distant peaks. Leaving his brother and his two sons of seven and nine to help Rebecca with the farming, he made his bold way over those peaks, stopping at the site of the present town of Boone to camp, then pushed on toward his goal.

At last the mighty hunter was on his way to that happy hunting-ground, the bluegrass meadows and canebrakes of Caintuck, alive with deer, bear, buffalo, and hostile Shawnees. But hostile Indians could not keep Daniel Boone from following the course toward which he had been traveling for thirty-five years, the course that was leading him to a hunter's paradise. Nothing could keep him any longer from answering the call of the lure of a distant land.

A PALACE AND A WAR

WHEN GOVERNOR WILLIAM TRYON ARRIVED FROM ENGLAND IN 1764 with his wife and four-year-old daughter, he found no house provided for the governor of the colony of North Carolina to live in. For a while, he stayed at Brunswick Town in a residence he called Castle Tryon.

Governor Tryon worried because there was no permanent capital city. Meetings of the peoples' Assembly were held here and there, and the public records were carried about in carts from place to place. This was a sad state of affairs, he thought. He decided to put the capitol, the mass of public records, and the governor's residence all in one place. He chose New Bern, because it was halfway between the settlements along Albemarle Sound in the northeast and the towns of Brunswick and Wilmington in the southeast. He seemed not to worry about the poor small farmers who lived far away to the west.

Governor Tryon wanted to build a large, handsome house—one of which the colony could be proud. He wanted it to be the most elegant structure in all the American colonies. John Hawks, an architect who had come with Tryon from England, was asked to plan a Palace that would look like the beautiful homes back in England.

Work began in 1767. The building was to be constructed of brick and trimmed in marble. The architect went to Philadelphia to get workmen, and the new Palace began to rise. The main building was two stories above a large basement. Curving off from the main building were covered walkways leading to small side wings. This plan allowed for a courtyard facing the streets of New Bern. In the back was a lawn that stretched down to the banks of the wide Trent River.

Metalworkers came from London to install the lead gutters, and mantles were ordered from England. So sturdy were the brick buildings that when a hurricane with 100-mile gales struck New Bern causing great destruction and killing six people, no harm was done to the Palace.

After three years of work, Tryon moved into the main building and put his family on the second floor. Mostly the first floor was used for offices and a meeting place for the Assembly. In the small east wing the public records were stored, and a kitchen and a laundry were there too. The west wing was used as a stable, and the grooms had their quarters on the second floor.

On December 5, 1770, Governor Tryon gave a grand ball to celebrate the opening of the Palace. The Assembly was meeting there for the first time. In the evening, Governor and Mrs. Tryon sat in two large armchairs in the great hall and received hundreds of guests. A bonfire was lighted on the grounds and fireworks brightened the sky. Food and drink were provided for all who came, both those who could get into the crowded Palace and those who had to remain outside. It was a great occasion, and Governor Tryon was proud to have built for North Carolina the most handsome building in all the colonies.

Now, it may seem strange, but not every North Carolinian was proud of the Palace, and especially was this true of those poor small farmers who lived far away in the western part of the state. Tryon Palace had cost a lot of money, and it was up to the taxpayers all over the colony to foot the bill. To them, the building was a great luxury for a poor colony like North Carolina, and they resented both Tryon and his costly Palace.

In this matter, the western farmers were unlike the well-to-do eastern planters, who could visit the Palace and enjoy it. The poor farmers did not have the money to take a long trip to New Bern, where they would have felt out-of-place, anyway, among such rich surroundings.

For some time the small farmers in and around Hillsborough and Salisbury had been complaining about their tax troubles. Some of the government tax collectors tricked the people into paying more than was due. After all, the farmers had little ready money. They raised good cattle and crops but had few handy markets where they could sell them.

Once, when a farmer could not pay his tax, the government agent came and took away his horse to sell for the tax debt. This was a terrible thing to happen, for when a farmer lost his horse, he had no means of transportation.

When his friends heard about it, they gathered together and went to Hillsborough. They called themselves Regulators because they had decided to "regulate" their affairs if the government would not do it for them. In Hillsborough they got back the horse, the saddle, and the bridle. Then they roamed about the town as mad as they could be and fired some shots into the tax collector's house.

The small western farmers were angry also, because of the heavy poll tax they had to pay for building Tryon Palace. A poll tax is a tax on every man who votes, and it did not trouble the eastern planters, but the western farmers did not have much money. Finally, they decided they would not pay the tax at all. Governor Tryon tried to straighten out this bad situation, but he had no luck. After the incident of the farmer's horse, the Regulators were so bold that they swept down on Hillsborough once more, beat up the lawyers in the courthouse, ran the judge from his courtroom, and dragged the tax collector through the streets of the town.

Though the farmers may have been right in protesting the tax, Governor Tryon could not stand by while they rioted and broke the laws. Such disgraceful conduct had to be stopped. So he called together the militia, as the soldiers from each county were called, and marched on Hillsborough to put an end to the disorders. On May 16, 1771, with two field cannons, six swivel guns mounted on carriages, and a thousand men, he faced two thousand Regulators near Alamance Creek west of Hillsborough.

He sent word for them to return to their homes or be fired on. The reply came, "Fire away then!" Tryon gave the order to fire, but his soldiers hesitated. Raising himself up from his saddle, he shouted, "Fire! Fire on them, or fire on me!"

The Battle of Alamance began. But the Regulators, without organization and without heavy artillery, were no match for the governor's well-trained troops. In two hours it was all over, the unhappy and misguided Regulators in retreat. Later, near Hillsborough, six of the Regulator leaders were hanged. Then victorious Governor Tryon returned to New Bern, where a noisy welcome greeted him at the Palace, the very building that had helped cause the War of the Regulation.

The oppressed but law-breaking Regulators had lost the war, but all America remembered how the poor taxpayers hated the payment of any taxes for which they did not vote themselves.

Years later, an old servant went into the basement of Tryon Palace to look for some eggs hidden in the hay there. She carried a candle that fell into the hay. Shortly, the whole Palace was aflame. It was midnight, February 27, 1798, when the most beautiful building in America was destroyed.

Today, however, handsome Tryon Palace with its two wings and its gardens and its courtyard has been rebuilt in all its glory. One may walk from room to room and see it just as it was in Governor Tryon's day. One may also visit the site of the Battle of Alamance near Burlington.

THE HORNET'S NEST

LORD CORNWALLIS WAS A PROUD ENGLISH NOBLEMAN WHO, AFTER
being educated at Eton, came to America to fight for the
British during the Revolutionary War. He was short and
thick-set, like a bulldog, and he was determined that the
people of North Carolina would obey the government of
George III back in London. He was a brave man, too, as
brave as he was proud.

But just as brave and proud were the people of Charlotte Town and Mecklenburg County. They had no use
for George III, or Lord Cornwallis either, for that matter.
In May, 1775, more than a year before the Declaration of
Independence in Philadelphia on July 4, 1776, the people
in Charlotte Town and in the country near it had a meeting. At this meeting they declared their hatred for British
rulers across the Atlantic Ocean.

Lord Cornwallis had a grand plan to defeat the American people who wanted independence. Starting deep in the South, he would move northward. On the way he would get help from those still loyal to the King and fight those who were not loyal. He had been told that, especially around Charlotte Town, he would meet with many Loyalists devoted to George III. How false the report was he was soon to discover.

The year was 1780, the month September. Cornwallis had just won a great battle in South Carolina, and he was sure of continued success. Charlotte Town would be the base of his campaign to subdue the whole state of North Carolina. On the morning of September 26, Cornwallis was near the town, ready to enter it with glory. He had no doubts that the people would welcome him and his large army of battle-tried Redcoats with many wagons of supplies.

In 1780, Charlotte Town was a tiny village of only two streets, named Trade and Tryon. Where the two streets crossed was a large building set on eight pillars, twelve feet from the ground. This was the courthouse. There were two stairways leading up to a porch at the front door. The open space underneath the courthouse was used as a market where farmers came to sell their products. And at the back of the open space, between the brick pillars, was a stone wall three or four feet high.

Along with the courthouse, Charlotte Town had just a few homes, mostly log huts, scattered up and down the two dusty streets. Only one house was painted. There was a jail, a store, a tavern, and a school. Fewer than a hundred people lived in the village, but prosperous farmers tilled the rich lands nearby. Between the cleared fields of the farms were heavy, thick woods. What attracted Cornwallis, especially, were a number of grist mills in the county. He planned to use these for grinding grain into flour for his soldiers.

On that morning of September 26, Cornwallis probably expected a committee to come from town to greet him. Instead, at the edge of the village, his advance troops were fired on by militiamen (local soldiers kept at home for the protection of the county), who then quickly disappeared into the thick forests. Cornwallis was puzzled. He had been told that the people of Mecklenburg, like the Scottish soldiers of Flora Macdonald, were to be his friends.

Since he was a cautious commander, he sent a group of Redcoats forward to find out how matters went. As this group neared the courthouse, they were greeted by a burst of fire. Some twenty Americans on horseback had hidden behind the stone wall underneath the courthouse, ready for the British. The Redcoats fell back.

Cornwallis' pride was hurt. He left the safety of his command post, galloped into the village, and shouted to his soldiers to follow. Two more charges were made, with the Americans firing from their position behind the wall. At that point, heavily outnumbered, they slipped away into the deep woods. It was only then that Cornwallis occupied Charlotte Town, angered that his large British army had been halted by a mere handful of American sharpshooters.

Lord Cornwallis set up his headquarters at the home of Colonel Thomas Polk, across the street from the courthouse. The next day, September 27, he issued a proclamation for all of the people of Charlotte Town and Mecklenburg to give up their firearms and to stay peacefully at their homes under the protection of the King's army. He was baffled when only a few came forward to turn over their guns.

Lord Cornwallis needed supplies for his huge army, now moving north with the hope of conquering all America. His messengers went to the farmers with a promise that soldiers would arrive at the farms to buy supplies. Until then, the farmers were to stay where they were.

But the independent, liberty-loving farmers of Mecklenburg paid no attention to the general's orders. They hid their produce and deserted their homes. They did not want British money. Instead, they shot at the Redcoats from hiding.

After a while, Cornwallis' supplies were dwindling. This was true, even though he had captured Colonel Thomas Polk's mill. There he had found 28,000 pounds of flour and a quantity of wheat. To feed his army, Cornwallis had one hundred cattle killed each day. His soldiers dreaded riding around the county and going into the farm yards. One of his messengers said he could not ride anywhere safely, because he found the "enemy concealed along every pathway."

One particularly unhappy expedition came on October 3. A large party of 450 cavalry led forty wagons up to a rich farm. The place was deserted, but some grain was left behind in the farm buildings. The Redcoats were merry. They sicked the dogs on the chickens. They overturned a beehive, and the bees swarmed out to chase the howling soldiers all over the yard. Soldiers began loading the wagons with grain. Amid the confusion, a red-faced British captain stood smiling in the doorway of the house. Perhaps he remembered his general's promise to pay the farmer with British money, but the farmer was nowhere to be seen.

The farmer, as a matter of fact, was one of fourteen Americans hidden in nearby trees. As he watched with bitterness the theft of his belongings, his anger exploded and he whispered to his friends:

"I can't wait any longer. Let everyone pick his man. The red-face captain is mine."

Shots rang out. Dogs, chickens, Redcoats, and cattle ran in circles or tried to find a hiding place. Those near the road started a hasty retreat. As they raced the eight miles back to Charlotte Town, patriot militiamen along the way peppered them with bullets. A few Redcoats dropped beside the road. Back at the meeting of Trade and Tryon streets, some of the weary horses fell dead at the steps leading up to the second floor of the courthouse.

As he talked with his officers, Cornwallis complained of the terrible situation in Mecklenburg County. He remarked on the strange way things had gone in Charlotte Town, for he had expected friends there. Now he had to admit that, though Charlotte Town was "an agreeable village," it was, at least for him, a "hornet's nest." One of his officers remarked that the people of the county "were more hostile to England" than any other people in America.

Even so, Lord Cornwallis felt rather safe. To protect his flanks, he had smaller armies to the east and west. The one to the west was under the command of Major Patrick Ferguson.

Then, late on the rainy afternoon of Saturday, October 7, a messenger rode down the muddy road into Charlotte Town with bad news. It was far worse news than the rout of 450 of his best British cavalrymen by fourteen American farmers. The messenger reported that American pioneers from the hill country had soundly defeated Major Ferguson's army at Kings Mountain to the west. The major himself had been killed. Lord Cornwallis was terrified; his base at Charlotte Town was unprotected on the left. He knew that he must turn around and retreat into South Carolina. He must get out of the way of the stinging hornets he had found in North Carolina.

Some days later, the roads still muddy from the autumn rains, Lord Cornwallis issued marching orders. He was in a hurry, so much in a hurry that he left twenty wagons of equipment behind him, as well as tents, clothing, and guns. Also left behind were bodies of his soldiers buried in the yard of Liberty Hall. This was a school, two blocks from the courthouse, which had been used as a hospital for the sick Redcoats.

Cornwallis, as he turned to the south, was ill too. At a secure distance from the hornet's nest at Charlotte Town, he paused two days to recover from a dangerous fever. Then he hurried on.

The first British invasion of North Carolina had been a dismal failure. Cornwallis' plan for the conquest of all America had fallen to pieces during the fifteen days he had spent inside the hornet's nest.

Lord Cornwallis was a brave and determined man. After several months of rest, he led his army once more into North Carolina, where he began chasing the poorly armed American forces under General Nathanael Greene. When Greene finally stood his ground at Guilford Courthouse (near present-day Greensboro), he was no match for the bully Cornwallis. Cornwallis won the Battle of Guilford Courthouse, the greatest battle fought on the soil of North Carolina during the Revolutionary War. But the British victory came at such a cost, and so many of his best soldiers were killed, that he no longer had a powerful army. A year after his visit to the hornet's nest, he faced General George Washington at Yorktown, Virginia, and surrendered.

America had won its independence from England at last.

FLORA MACDONALD

NOT ALL OF THE PEOPLE OF NORTH CAROLINA WERE EAGER FOR independence from Great Britain. Some were quite willing to remain under the rule of King George III. Instead of fighting against England, they wanted to fight *for* the Mother Country. Because of this, they were called Loyalists.

Many Loyalists lived along the upper Cape Fear River, and in and around Cross Creek, where Fayetteville is now located. Most of these Loyalists had come to America from the mountains of Scotland and were called Scottish Highlanders. The most famous of them was a woman called Flora Macdonald.

The reason the Scottish Highlanders were loyal to Great Britain makes a strange story. Once they had fought against the English king. Then, in defeat, they swore an oath never again to oppose him. Even after they came to North Carolina, they remembered their oath.

There was, too, another matter. In North Carolina, the King had provided them with large grants of land on which to farm. They thought that, if they fought King George III and lost, their lands would be taken from them. So, when troubles started with England, the Scottish Highlanders were determined to stand with the King.

Flora Macdonald's story is a strange one also. Many years before, in Scotland, when the Highlanders had fought against England, Flora had become a heroine. At that time the Scots did not like the grandfather of King George III who then ruled, and they wanted the throne for their own Scotsman, Bonnie Prince Charlie. They fought a battle and, as we know, the Scotsmen lost.

While the English soldiers looked everywhere, Bonnie Prince Charlie hid in the valleys and caves of the mountains. A large sum of money was offered for his capture. Just as he was about to be captured, Flora Macdonald saved his life. She dressed up Bonnie Prince Charlie as a servant woman and he walked past the English soldiers in this disguise. She took him to her mother's house on a distant island, from which Bonnie Prince Charlie escaped to France.

Flora Macdonald was a pretty young woman and well educated. Though she was quite small in stature, she was not afraid as she walked by the English soldiers with her tall "servant woman." For this act of bravery, the Scottish Highlanders loved her.

But the English did not forget how she had helped Bonnie Prince Charlie escape. They arrested her and put her in the Tower of London. She was freed a year later but all of her land was taken from her by the English. After a few years she married Allan Macdonald and raised a family. They lived very poorly in Scotland, so after about twenty years they decided to start a new life somewhere else.

They emigrated from Scotland to North Carolina, where so many other Highlanders were already living. They swore, too, that they would never again fight the English King.

When the Macdonalds arrived at the port of Wilmington in 1774, Flora was no longer a young woman. Some of her children were married and had stayed back in England. She was now past fifty years old, but still she had a flashing eye and a youthful appearance. Her fame as the one who had saved Bonnie Prince Charlie had never dimmed, and she was the best-known woman of all Scotland.

In Wilmington, a grand ball was given in her honor. Then Allan Macdonald and she took a boat up the Cape Fear River to Cross Creek, where a Scottish band greeted them. They were welcomed into the best homes of Cross Creek. When Allan and his son went out to look for a plantation, Flora and her daughter stayed on in Cross Creek.

Finally they settled at "Killiegrey," a plantation west of Cross Creek. There was a house already there, a barn, a kitchen shed, a stable, a corn crib, and a grist mill, which ground the corn and brought in enough money to feed the entire family. For Flora, it looked as if she had found a peaceful spot to live out her remaining years. She and her family were very happy.

But peace and happiness were not to last long. Hardly had they begun to improve their plantation than word came from Charlotte Town of troubles brewing. Then Allan got a message to round up all the Loyalists he could find and come to Cross Creek. What were he and Flora to do? They would abide by their oath, of course. This time they would fight *for* the king, not against him.

In February of 1776, the Loyalists gathered at Cross

Creek, some 1500 of them. Allan was one of the leaders, and Flora was with him there. The Loyalists were to march to Wilmington, a patriot stronghold.

At Cross Creek, Flora mounted a white horse and reviewed the troops. As she rode up and down the lines of soldiers, they were in high spirits. They sang the old Scottish songs. Flags were waving, drums beating, bagpipes playing. It was a great day. Flora kept to her horse, speaking to a soldier here, another soldier there. As they marched out of Cross Creek, Flora went with them.

Remembering the days of Bonnie Prince Charlie long ago, Flora wanted to stay with them all the way to Wilmington. But her husband said it would not be safe for her and ordered her back. She embraced him, tears in her eyes, then rode by her soldiers once more. At last, she galloped away to "Killiegrey" on her white horse. It was a sad moment. Flora had no way of knowing that she would not again see Allan till many years later in Scotland.

A week or so after leaving her husband, Flora Macdonald heard the bad news. At Moore's Creek Bridge on the road to Wilmington, the Scottish Highlander army had been surprised by a smaller patriot force and badly defeated. More than half the Highlanders had been captured and put in prison, including Flora's husband Allan, their son Alexander, and the husband of their daughter Anne.

Flora Macdonald did not know where to turn. First she was questioned by patriot officers. Then "Killiegrey" was ransacked and finally taken away from her. For a while she stayed in the home of friends. The seasons passed. Allan was still in prison, and North Carolina was not a place where she could prosper and find peace. After five years in the state, she got permission to return to Scotland. To buy her passage from Wilmington, she sold her handsome silver dishes and other personal belongings.

Everything had been taken from her—except her bravery and her high spirits. On the voyage back to Scotland, her ship was attacked by a French vessel. Instead of hiding in her cabin, she stayed on deck while the battle raged, old as she was. Her arm was broken, but she remained on deck, encouraging the sailors in their fight.

North Carolina has never forgotten this famous woman, who did what she thought was right even when the odds were against her. In Scotland she was later joined by her husband, and when she died, she was buried in the bed sheets that Bonnie Prince Charlie had slept on that night in her mother's house. She had carried them with her everywhere. They were about all she had left.

Today, Cross Creek has long since had its name changed to Fayetteville. North of Wilmington is the site of the Battle of Moore's Creek Bridge, now a national park.

HOECAKE FOR BREAKFAST

ON MAY 30, 1791, THE HOUSEHOLD AT BRANDON PLANTATION IN
Rowan County was astir at dawn. The master of the house,
Richard Brandon, Esq., had ridden his finest bay mare the
six miles south to Salisbury the evening before, and Mistress
Brandon was to depart in the coach at sunup to attend the
great celebration.

Betsey sat dejectedly on a stool in the airy bedroom,
watching her mother get ready. The blue satin gown, with
lace overskirt and rose-colored underdress, the white silken
slippers with tiny high heels, and the fine, cobwebby lace
shawl were all laid out on the big bed. Tildy, the maid,
was dressing Mistress Brandon's hair in the latest fashion
with high pompadour, puffs and curls, and snowy white
powder.

"Don't look so mournful, child," Mistress Brandon said to Betsey. "I know you are disappointed, and I'm sorry as can be."

"It's not fair," cried Betsey, kicking her red shoes on the polished floor. "I'm no child either. I'm thirteen years old, quite grown up. I think it's mean of you and father not to let me go to Salisbury and meet President Washington."

"Why, Betsey! What a fit of temper!" exclaimed Mistress Brandon. "You know why you cannot go. There's measles in town, and we can't risk your getting it. Remember, your brother died of measles years ago." She wiped away a tear and patted her face with the goose-down powder puff. "Nothing would make me happier, darling, than to have you ride beside me in the coach in the parade, and sit between your father and me at the noonday banquet, but I don't dare take you."

Betsey dabbed at her eyes and burst out, "I don't care if I do catch the old measles! I want to see the president." Then, noting her mother's stricken look, she changed her tone. "Oh, Mama, I'm sorry. I didn't mean to sound so horrid. But I do so much want to meet President Washington. Everyone says he's such a fine figure of a man, with his handsome velvet clothes and his golden coach."

Just then the sound of wheels grated on the circular driveway in front of the mansion, and Betsey jumped up. "Here's Pompey with the coach, already, Mama. I'll help fasten your gown." She started hooking up the fine blue satin dress. "You look beautiful, Mama. You'll take in everything, won't you, and tell me all about General Washington when you get back?"

"Of course I will, darling," Mistress Brandon replied,

kissing Betsey's tear-stained cheek. "I'll bring you a souvenir. I'll tuck a candy into my pocket for you. We're sure to have all kinds of sweets on the banquet table." She swept from the room, through the broad hall, and out the wide front door, followed slowly by Betsey in her blue calico dress. Mistress Brandon mounted the steps of the coach and waved to Betsey as she drove away. Betsey waved back, then she turned and burst into tears. "I wanted to see the president," she sobbed, leaning against the carved doorframe.

"Now, now, Miss Betsey." Betsey felt the comforting arm of Charity, the cook, around her shoulder and heard her soothing voice. "Quit your frettin', chile. Come on to the kitchen house and help Charity with the churnin'. I'll bake some fresh hoecake, and when the butter comes, I'll lay you a snack under the trees, where it's nice and cool. You got up mighty early this morning, and you'll be hungry again, soon."

"Who wants old hoecake?" Betsey sneered, as she followed Charity around the house to the kitchen. "I wanted to dine with the president." She dropped down in a splint-bottomed chair beside the kitchen-house door, grabbed the churn dasher, and started pumping it up and down. Her gray-striped kitten tried to play with her red shoe-ribbons, but she kicked at him. "Go away, Puffball," she said crossly. "You don't even care that Mama and Father are in Salisbury dining with the president, and I have to stay home and churn."

She pounded the dasher so furiously that droplets of milk flew up from the hole in the churn lid and splattered on her hands. When the kitten jumped to her lap to lick at them, she pushed him away again. "Go on," she muttered, "and leave me alone."

Betsey sloshed the dasher, up and down, up and down, feeling sorrier for herself every minute, until the drops of milk began to turn to little blobs of yellow butter.

"Charity, the butter is ready," Betsey called and dashed away so the cook wouldn't see her tears. "I'm going to find Puffball. He's probably catching a bird, or something, the naughty thing." She fled to the front of the house, but instead of looking for the kitten, flopped down on the broad steps of the porch and sulked.

Suddenly she heard a noise down on the highroad, at the end of the long, tree-bordered driveway that led to the mansion, and she shaded her eyes to try to see better the coach stopped there and the commotion of people milling about. "Charity!" she called. "Come quickly, there's something amiss on the highroad."

"What is it, Miss Betsey?" Charity asked, panting up to her. "Well, land sakes! Look at that old broken-down coach. Must be some plain traveler. Here comes a man up the lane. You give him welcome, chile, while I go back and tend to my butter. Better dry them tears away. Your mama'd be 'shamed to have a stranger see you cryin'."

"I'm not crying," Betsey snapped. She stood on the steps, watching as a tall, oldish man trudged up the lane between the two rows of big oak trees. He was plainly dressed in brown linen, with white stockings, though the silver buckles on his shoes shone brightly, and the buttons on his coat gleamed in the early morning sunlight. At least he's a gentleman, Betsey thought. But why does he have to stop here?

As the gentleman neared Betsey, she was still scowling, but he did not appear to notice. He lifted his hat and made her a sweeping bow. "Good morning, little lady," he said. "What a nice, cool grove you have here. When my coach threw a wheel just now, I decided to stroll up to your house and ask if I might rest a bit. I'm very weary."

Betsey wiped her face with her sleeve and made him a stiff curtsy. "You're welcome, sir."

"Thank you, my dear. It is a hot day, isn't it?"

Betsey hoped the gentleman thought she was only wiping her face because of the heat and had not noticed she'd been crying. "Come into the house, sir, and rest in the parlor. My parents are in Salisbury, to greet the president," she explained. "I so wanted to go, but I had to stay at home. They do say President Washington is the finest, handsomest gentleman who ever lived, and that he dresses in velvet and lace and rides in a golden coach. I'm disappointed not to see him. Have you ever seen Mr. Washington?"

"Yes, indeed, many times. And I assure you he is just a plain, tired, gray-headed old man. He dresses up on occasion, when he must, but his coach is not golden. On state occasions he rides in a cream-colored coach, trimmed in red, but when he travels he uses a plain coach like other people. If you do not mind, I will not go in. I prefer staying outside, in the shade of your fine trees, until my coach is mended."

"Then come around the house, where there are seats," Betsey invited the traveler.

As the gentleman seated himself on a bench at the rear of the house, he said, "Perhaps you will give me a bite of breakfast. I have come far, and I have a long, hard time ahead." He sighed deeply and momentarily closed his eyes.

"Oh, sir, please excuse me!" Betsey suddenly forgot her own disappointment in concern for the tired-looking gentleman. "I'm sorry to be so unmannerly. My mother would be ashamed of me. I have just churned some fresh butter, and Charity is baking hoecake on the kitchen hearth, but that is too plain for company. If you can wait we will cook you something better."

"Oh, hoecake and buttermilk are fit fare for a king—or a president." The gentleman smiled. "I hope you will join me in the meal."

Betsey scurried about, bringing out her mother's best plates, goblets, and silver and laying the yard table with linen, while Charity scrambled eggs to serve with the hoecake.

When they had finished eating, the gentleman rose, washed his hands at the well, then kissed Betsey on the forehead. "My, that was a fine breakfast," he said. "Never have I tasted better hoecake, thanks to your excellent cook, Charity. The fresh butter and buttermilk were delicious beyond words, and eaten in the company of such a charming little hostess. Why, the banquet in Salisbury cannot be half so pleasing. I haven't learned your name, my dear."

"Betsey Brandon, sir," Betsey said, shy at the gentleman's praise. "Oh, this was nothing sir. How fine it would have been to go to Salisbury and dine at the banquet with the president." Her tone was wistful. "Are you going there, sir? Will you see President Washington?"

"Yes, Mistress Betsey," the tall man answered. "From there I shall go on to Salem, a town celebrated for its welcome to strangers, but I am sure I shall not ever meet with more hospitality than you have shown me here. Now I must go."

As the gentleman stepped briskly down the lane toward his coach, he turned and waved his hat to the watching Betsey. "The compliments of President George Washington to Mistress Betsey Brandon, the finest little hostess in Carolina," he called out, then hurried on.

Betsey stood for a moment without moving, then she sped back to the kitchen shouting, "Charity! Oh, Charity! I have dined with the president! I have dined with President Washington. And Charity! He kissed me, too!"

THE STATE CAPITOL
IN RALEIGH

THE MOST IMPORTANT BUILDING IN NORTH CAROLINA, AND SOME say the most beautiful, is the State Capitol in Raleigh. It is the second Capitol to be built on the site, for the first one was burned.

For several years after the Revolutionary War, North Carolina had no one capital city. The lawmakers moved about from town to town, meeting in first one building and then another. In 1792, however, a piece of land in a thick forest near the center of the state was chosen as the future capital city. The spot was named Raleigh, though there was no town yet, just the forest. Late in the same year, workers cut down some trees and started building a Capitol in the middle of the wooded area. A few people put up houses near the building, and the city of Raleigh began.

It took two years to complete this first Capitol, constructed of bricks made of clay found nearby. Though not a pretty building, it was much used. When the lawmakers were not meeting there, it was the place where actors put on plays, and performers walked on wires strung across the auditorium. Dances were held there on one day, and it served as a "church" on another.

Some time later, North Carolina made a lot of improvements in its Capitol. The people of the state wanted a prettier building because they had ordered an expensive statue of George Washington made by the noted Italian sculptor Canova to be placed in it. When the statue reached Raleigh, it was said to be the most valuable work of art in the entire United States.

But Canova's handsome marble statue did not bring luck to the Capitol. Ten years after it was installed in the building—greatly admired by all who saw it—it was destroyed.

In June, 1831, when a tinsmith was repairing the roof, he accidently dropped some burning wood inside the building. Soon the whole structure was afire. It was a hot summer day, and there was no fire department to put out the flames. Citizens of Raleigh rushed around trying to save what they could. Official papers of the state were removed from the building, but the valuable books in the library were already being destroyed.

Everybody was worried about the Canova statue of George Washington. A brave lady, Miss Betsy Geddy, gathered a group of strong men about her. She cried for them to bring the statue out of the fiery place. While she yelled encouragement, the men tugged and tugged. But the marble was too heavy; they could not budge it. They had to leave it in the smoking rotunda.

Outside, they looked with horror while the seated figure

of our first President became red hot. Then the roof came crashing about it, and the valuable marble statue broke apart and crumbled to the floor.

Plans were soon made for a new Capitol. This time, the building would be larger and prettier. It would be patterned after the handsome temples of ancient Greece. A foundation was put down, and a cornerstone was laid. Inside the hollow cornerstone were placed, among other things, a Bible, copies of the constitutions of the state and the nation, and some coins. They are still there today.

Stonemasons came from Scotland to cut the granite blocks. The quarry, only a mile east of Capitol Square, was reached by a small railroad, the first in North Carolina. Horses drew the cars loaded with the big blocks of granite along the tracks of the railroad. On Sundays, the horses were not allowed to rest. The stonemasons invited ladies and gentlemen to ride up and down the early railroad.

In 1840, after seven years of construction, the new State Capitol was finished. Today, over a hundred years later, the outside of the structure is the same as it was then. The granite blocks have aged to a beautiful softness, which changes in color with the seasons. When snow is on the ground, the building has a bluish tinge. In spring, the granite is almost pink in color. In summer, the Capitol seems to be a greenish-brown. At night, all during the year, when the Capitol is floodlighted, the stone appears orange.

The building looks peaceful and comfortable set in the middle of a grove of tall oak trees. Yet, in the past, it has known troublesome times. During the Civil War, when northern troops marched into Raleigh, officials of the state met the enemy general and surrendered the city. The general promised that he would not allow the building to be destroyed, and he kept his word. Many capitol buildings in other southern states were burned to the ground.

There is a legend that when the northern soldiers entered Raleigh, one Confederate spy did not escape the town. He hid in a secret room in the Capitol, and he could not be found. For days and days he stayed there. This was believed to be only a legend for a long time. But many years later, when the inside of the building was being repaired, several small hidden rooms were discovered. Perhaps the legend has some truth to it.

In the center of the building is the rotunda, a large round area going all the way to the dome crowning the building. A visitor, climbing to the second floor, will notice nicks in the stone steps. Perhaps these nicks were made during the stormy days after the Civil War. At that time, it is said, whiskey barrels were rolled up the steps for the rowdy crowd then occupying the Capitol.

The second floor has halls where the legislature once met. On the ground floor are the offices of the Governor and other state leaders.

Among the oak trees and beside the paths that surround the Capitol, a visitor can find statues of some of North Carolina's great men, including three presidents of the United States. Near the Capitol are the Art Museum, the Legislative Building, the Museum of Natural History, and the Museum of History. In the Museum of History is a model of Canova's famous statue of George Washington that was burned in 1831.

THE GOLDEN DOORSTOP

JOHN REED, A HIRED GERMAN SOLDIER IN THE REVOLUTIONARY War, did not return to his homeland after the struggle. He settled on a small farm of his own in Cabarrus County and married a neighbor girl. One sunny Sunday morning in 1799, Mr. and Mrs. Reed set out for church, riding double on their only horse. As it was too far to walk, they left their three children at home. Conrad was thirteen, and Margaret and Johnny were younger. "Be good, children, and don't get into any mischief," Mrs. Reed called as they rode away.

When their parents were out of sight Conrad said, "Fetch my bow and arrow, Johnny, and let's shoot fish in Meadow Creek. You needn't trail along, Margaret. Fishing's for boys."

"I am coming, too," Margaret replied. "I can shoot a bow and arrow as well as you can."

"M-mm," grunted Conrad. "You'd better get barefooted, though, and not get your Sunday shoes all muddy."

Margaret sat down in the doorway of the cabin and took

off her black leather slippers and fine-knitted white stockings.

Then she jumped up to follow the boys. "Johnny, wait for me," she called, tucking the flowing overskirt of her blue-flowered gown into her belt. "Wait for me!"

"Aw, catch up if you can." Conrad sprinted across the pasture toward the creek that babbled between two rows of green willows. He and Johnny laughed at their sister's efforts to keep up.

The boys sat down on a boulder beside a pool in the stream where they knew the fish were swimming. Margaret ran up panting and flopped down beside them. She started to speak but Conrad shushed her with a frown.

The three of them remained as still as a fallen wind for a few moments, their eyes on the pool. Suddenly Johnny pointed to a shadow in its depths.

Twang! Conrad's arrow hit the water and the fish darted away.

"Missed it!" he said in disgust. "Margaret, you can get my arrow for me."

"Get it yourself, mister," Margaret answered, saucily. "I came to shoot fish, not chase after arrows."

"Johnny, make yourself useful and get my arrow," Conrad commanded.

"Aw, Con," Johnny complained, but he waded out carefully toward the arrow embedded in the sand.

"Get a move on, or that fish will never come back."

Johnny waded from the stream with the arrow in his chubby hand. "Now it's my turn to shoot."

"It is not, it's mine," Margaret stated.

"You're nothing but a girl," Johnny informed her. "Girls can't shoot straight."

"Just be quiet, will you?" Conrad said. "I'll shoot this time to settle the argument. Whoever brings in that arrow can have the next turn."

The three gazed into the pool again. After a few moments Conrad raised his bow and shot another barb. "Got him!" He jumped into the creek, splashing water to his waist, and made for the arrow bobbing about in the pool in the side of the flopping fish. Margaret and Johnny sloshed after him, but he was too quick and flung the fish and arrow to the grassy bank.

"I get the next shot, too," Conrad cried. "You two had better get in the sun and dry off, or Mother will skin you alive. You're soaking wet."

Conrad shot a third time, but his arrow struck something hard, its head broke off, and the shaft started floating downstream. He went after the shaft, but hit his big toe so hard on a stone that he cried out in pain.

"Drat that rock!" he exclaimed. "I nearly broke my toe on it." He tried to move the stone with his good foot, but could not budge it. He rolled up a sleeve and reached down to pick up the rock, but could not lift it with one hand.

Then he let out a shrill whistle. "Hey! Margaret, Johnny! Come look at this funny rock. It's not very big but it surely is heavy. Oh, well, no use bothering with it." He started wading downstream after his arrow shaft.

"It's real pretty," Margaret said. "It would make a good doorstop for Mother to use in place of her smoothing iron."

"That old yellow rock is too little for a doorstop," said

Johnny. He waded out and sat down on the bank of the creek.

Conrad splashed back to Margaret, who was trying to loosen the rock from the creek bed. "Look, Margaret, the point broke off my arrow when it hit that stone."

"Help me get it up. I want to take it home for Mother."

"Guess I might as well. We've scared off all the fish anyway." Conrad bent into the water and, using both hands, got the rock to the edge of the stream. "Grab it, Margaret, don't let it roll back."

Margaret and Johnny both grabbed for the rock and managed to hold it.

Conrad waded painfully from the stream. "Let a man lift it," he boasted, reaching down to pick up the prize. "Un—nn—." Grunting with the effort, he finally lifted the rock with both hands. "Well! I never saw a rock like this before. Look what a queer dullish yellow color it is."

"It will be real pretty to hold the cook-room door open," Margaret said. "Johnny, get our fish and let's go home. The folks will be back soon."

When Mr. and Mrs. Reed arrived home, they praised the children for catching a fine fish, and Mrs. Reed thanked them for her new doorstop.

During the next three years, while the stone lay on the kitchen floor, Mr. Reed remarked several times, "That certainly is an unusual piece of stone. It's so heavy for its size. Sometimes I think it might be more than just a piece of creek rock. But what? Mr. Atkinson, the silversmith in town, says it's nothing more."

Then one day Mr. Reed had to go to Fayetteville on

business. He took Conrad along, and Conrad suggested they take the doorstop and show it to a jeweler there.

"I don't think this is just an ordinary rock, Mr. Reed," the jeweler said, hefting the stone in his hands and scraping at it with his pocket knife. "I think it may contain some metal of one kind or another. I'll be glad to test it for you. You and the boy stop in tomorrow on your way home, and we'll see what we have."

Before beginning their homeward journey, Mr. Reed and Conrad returned to the jeweler's.

"Well, here's your rock, Mr. Reed," said the jeweler. He showed them a six-inch-long bar of shiny yellow metal. "It weighed out at seventeen pounds before I melted it down and cast it. Name your price and I'll buy it."

"Looks as if it might be worth right much," Mr. Reed replied. "How about three dollars and a half in hard money?"

"Three dollars and a half, Father?" exclaimed Conrad. "All that money for a little old piece of creek rock?"

"I'll pay it," interrupted the jeweler before they could say more, and he counted out the money to John Reed.

"You know, friend Reed," smiled the jeweler, with a crafty gleam in his eye, "you have just sold me a bar of pure gold."

"Gold!" shouted John Reed. "Gold? You mean that rock we've been using for a doorstop these last three years is gold? Why, you're a cheating thief!"

"You sold it to me," reminded the jeweler. "You set the price, I didn't."

"Come on, son." John Reed was so angry he could

hardly control himself. "Come on, let's get back to Cabarrus and begin panning Meadow Creek."

They hurried home, and at once began prospecting for more gold. With the help of slaves and others, they found nuggets weighing from one grain to twenty-eight pounds.

Naturally, the news of a gold strike in North Carolina leaked out and spread like fire on a dry prairie. It was the first gold ever found in the United States. Soon a large area in and around Cabarrus County was swarming with people from everywhere who were stricken with "gold fever."

John Reed realized the jeweler had cheated him by paying him only three dollars and a half for a nugget worth thousands. He sued the swindler for three thousand dollars and won his case, it is said.

From the time the first white men, French and Spanish, set foot on the soil of what is now Florida, on down through the periods of exploration, settlement, and colonization of our country, pioneers thought of, talked about, and searched for gold. No authentic records tell of their finding a single grain; nor did anyone find Indian relics made of the precious metal. It is not so strange, therefore, that John Reed and those who saw his doorstop failed to recognize it for what it really was, a nugget of almost pure gold. Since men had searched the land for the precious harvest for over two hundred years, they had just about given up the quest.

From 1803 until about sixty years later, North Carolina was known as The Golden State. More than fifty million dollars' worth of gold was taken from over three hundred mines in Montgomery, Cabarrus, Anson, Rowan, Randolph, Davidson, and Mecklenburg counties. People from many lands came to work the mines. Men, women, and children, free and slave, toiled from dawn to dusk. Everybody who could shake a pan or handle a pick seems to have descended upon that one section of North Carolina. A private mint was established in Rutherfordton by some Germans named Bechtler, and it was recognized by the United States government. The streets of Charlotte were said to have been paved with gold, because in the middle of the town there was a mine from which slag was taken and spread over the rough roads.

By the late 1820's the gold-producing area was found to extend into the Piedmont and up into the Blue Ridge Mountains. Great numbers of people were engaged in the ever-widening search. Then the lodes began to fail and miners drifted away. Gold was discovered in California in 1849 and men rushed there to stake claims. Civil strife became war in 1861, taking many men away, and the bonanza came to an end. The once-rich industry faded into a bare shade of its former vigorous self.

All that is left of the gold strike are the remains of some of the old mines—Bucktown, Brindletown, Gold Hill. Now and then an old prospector may be seen up in the hills, panning at some streamside for a bit of the glittering dust.

Few North Carolinians got rich from gold mining during the Golden Age of the Golden State. The cost of mining exceeded the profits, and dishonest out-of-state promoters made money by selling worthless claims for high prices. In the end the precious yellow metal did little for North Carolina beyond furnishing a short, but glorious, burst of excitement in the history of the state.

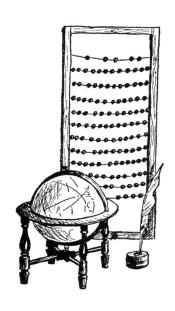

THE BOYS' ANSTALT
AT SALEM

NOTE FROM TIMOTHY VOGLER TO HIS FATHER, CHRISTOPH VOGLER, in the Congregation Town of Salem in Wachovia, North Carolina.

Salem, North Carolina
May 28, 1817.

My dear Father:

You have expressed a wish to read the essay that I have prepared for our yearly examination, describing our school. I am presenting it herewith, inscribed in my best handwriting, for your approval. It has been read and commended by our first teacher, Brother Johann Gottlieb Herman.

Respectfully yrs.
Timothy Vogler, aged 11 years.

[80]

THE BOYS' ANSTALT AT SALEM
by
Timothy Vogler, aged 11.

The Anstalt is the school, where we sleep, and where we learn the lessons that will fit us Little Boys to take our places in the Single Brethren's House when we reach the age of fourteen. It was dedicated to the glory of Our Lord, and to the education of His children, with a love feast and music by a choir of horns in the year 1794.

I shall first describe the building and the rules of the Anstalt. Then I shall tell of our activities and something of what has happened in Salem this year, 1817.

The Anstalt is a fine, large brick building, three stories high, with a tile roof, situated on the northeast corner of Salem Square. The first floor has four rooms, a hall, and a closet. On the right of the hall, in front, is the kitchen and dining-hall, with a large fireplace containing several cranes for kettles and a hearth for cooking-pots and pans. Back of the kitchen there is a storage room that is always cool because it is not above ground. On the left, in the front, is the room where the housefather lives, and back of it is the bakery containing a large stone and plaster oven. These rooms all have tile floors.

The second floor, which is reached by a pretty, curving stairway, has four classrooms, fitted out handsomely for their purposes, as well as a wide hall containing a new pianoforte. In one schoolroom there is a teacher's table and chair, a long table with six benches for the pupils, a bookcase filled with books, and a cupboard for the storage of supplies. In this room, also, there is a fine abacus, two globes of the world, pens, inkpots, slates, paper, and other necessities for the gaining of knowledge.

The adjoining classroom holds our old piano and other musical instruments, such as the violin, and music stands and cabinets. In this room we learn to sing and to play an instrument, as well as how to tune and take care of the same. We have classes in the two other rooms, and sometimes we gather in the hall for exercise.

The third floor, also reached by a curving stairway, is made into a sleeping-hall and sickroom, each well warmed by a pretty tiled stove. These rooms are furnished with beds, with comfortable straw sacks, chairs, and basins upon tables for washing our faces each morning. We bring our combs, soap, and towels from home.

Behind the Anstalt, and separated from it by a large yard, is a big, covered shed where the boys can play and a smaller shed for storing wood. Beyond the sheds are the gardens for growing herbs, vegetables, and flowers. Our Anstalt and its surroundings are indeed pleasant.

Now I shall give a summary of the rules of the Anstalt.

We rise at five or five-fifteen of the clock in spring and summer, and at six or six-thirty in fall and winter. In silence, under the eyes of an instructor, we wash and dress as neatly as we can and go home for breakfast. We must return by seven o'clock to make our beds, silently, with a teacher present, then study diligently until eight. At eight o'clock we commence lessons for the day. A teacher always reads the Daily Text, and we sing a verse before we begin classes.

My morning classes consist of arithmetic, English reading, German writing and orthography, and Latin on alternating days. I am finding English to be my most difficult subject, since we commonly use the German language in Wachovia.

We are dismissed at eleven o'clock if there is no Children's Meeting. If there is one, a teacher walks us into the hall for exercise, then back for the meeting. Afterwards, we go home to lunch but must return to school by half past twelve.

From half past twelve until three o'clock I have instruction in English writing, German reading and spelling, history, geography, and singing. On Wednesday afternoons we learn verses from the Scriptures, and on Fridays, German grammar. In our German reading we read from the I & II Chronicles in the Old Testament, the German Daily Text, and the Hymnbook. In English reading we use the English Daily Text and Noah Webster's *American Spelling Book*.

On Saturdays we do not have school, but we must shake out our straw sacks and sweep and clean the whole house.

Our penmanship classes are taught in script, both German and English, which we write on paper, with ink, instead of on slates as we do our arithmetic. Our teachers are very strict about neatness and the formation of letters. I am apt to make many blots and smudges so that I often have to rewrite whole exercises. I find this very discouraging.

The best part of our schoolday is three o'clock, when we run home for Vespers. Mother always has something good for me to eat for Vespers. I like her gingerbread best of anything.

Immediately after Vespers we return to school to study

until four o'clock, which is the hour for our walk. I will
say more about this fine, free time later.

When our walk is over at five, we go home for supper,
then back to the Anstalt to study, and to bed at eight or half
after, according to the time of year. Some evenings we must
sew or mend, as if we were girls. This chore is most unpleasant to all. We always sing a verse before we get into
bed.

When the time for our walk comes, we are always glad
if Brother Thomas Schulz accompanies us. Some days we
play roundball in the meadow, hunt for trilliums or other
wildflowers, or capture butterflies for our collections, fish
in the mill stream, or run races. On other fine days when
we do not take a walk, we fill the woodshed. We go home
at five o'clock to help our parents with the evening chores
and to eat supper.

On rainy or stormy days, or if the streets and lanes are
too muddy, we spend our free time in the Anstalt playing
chess or checkers, singing, or reading. We have many fine
books to choose from, written in Greek, French, Latin, German, and English. I am a poor Latin scholar, but I am
striving hard to improve my knowledge of English, so I
read English books.

At all times we are required to be orderly, clean, polite,
and respectful in our behavior. We must go about our tasks
quietly and properly. Cursing, swearing, and all kinds of
indecent language are prohibited, as well as fighting and
boxing. We are not allowed, at any time, to run about the
streets nor to fire guns, even on the Fourth of July. The
Church Elders frown mightily upon boisterous play of any
kind.

The Boarding School for Girls is a large establishment facing the Square a few paces from our Anstalt, but we are never allowed to mingle with the pupils there.

In the town this year we have had a plague of fever. Two of the pupils from the girls' school were called to their Heavenly Home by reason of the disease. They were buried in God's Acre nearby. Our Guardian Angels protected the boys in their Anstalt, for which we give humble thanks to our Saviour. Our second teacher, Brother Schulz, suffered at length from the fever, but in time he recovered his health.

Measles spread abroad in our community, and our sickroom was filled for a time, but all regained their normal spirits. Measles is a dreaded disease. It makes one feel most miserable.

A case of smallpox in a traveler gave the town such a fright that it was decreed that we must all be inoculated with cowpox. This was a most unpleasant operation, causing sore arms in all the boys, thus compelling them to give up playing roundball for a time. No one caught smallpox.

The Little Boys in Salem are fortunate to be living in this age, when the Elders of the Congregation hold their welfare in such high esteem as to provide them with this Anstalt.

This essay was written by Timothy Vogler, age 11 years, in May, 1817, and presented for the Public Examinations.

While the above story was not actually written by Timothy Vogler, he was a pupil at the Salem Boys' Anstalt in 1817, and he might have written just such an account of the school. This essay was compiled from translations of entries in boys' diaries of that year and from *Records of the Moravians in*

North Carolina, Vol. VII. At that period the Moravians were still using the German language.

Next to the church, the Moravian Brethren considered the education of their children, both girls and boys, of prime importance. Since the Moravians, even the school boys, kept very careful records and diaries, they left many detailed accounts of their various schools in each of the settlements in Wachovia. These records and diaries, which have been translated into English, give wonderfully detailed accounts of life in the Moravian settlements of Wachovia (now Forsyth County, North Carolina) from 1753 onward.

A boarding school for girls was established in Salem in 1772 and is still in operation as Salem College. First mention of a school for boys in Salem was made in 1771, five years after the founding of the town. This was a small school held in the house of Brother Aust, the potter. In 1773 a school in writing and arithmetic was held in the Single Brethren's House for the instruction of apprentices. It probably met at night, since the boys worked during the day at learning their trades. Salem, being the central town of Wachovia, was headquarters for the trades and crafts practiced by the Moravian brethren.

Accounts tell of several schools for "Little Boys" (under the apprentice age of fourteen) in Salem, until 1779 when an organized school was begun for the teaching of reading, writing, and arithmetic, with music, geography, geometry, and languages as secondary subjects. This school was held in several different locations until 1794, when the Anstalt, or home-school, was erected.

This building, now restored, still stands in the village of

Old Salem, just as it stood in 1817 when Timothy Vogler was a pupil there. It retains its original tile roof, some original floor (in the store room), and the original stairway to the second floor. One schoolroom is furnished as it was in Timothy's school days, and the remainder of the Anstalt, with an annex, has been made into a fascinating museum. The museum contains artifacts of the region from early Indian days, as well as objects used in daily life by the Moravians in Wachovia from 1753 until the present. Along with other buildings restored in Old Salem, this Anstalt is important in showing the development of education in our nation.

Many groups of school children from all over North Carolina and a great number of tourists from many places visit Old Salem, the restored Congregation Town, each year to see how one group of our ancestors lived and worked when the country was young.

CHEROKEE HERO

OLD TSALI, WEARING A BRIGHT TURBAN ABOVE HIS STRAGGLY black hair and a striped shirt tucked into buckskin trousers, lounged against a post on the porch of his plank cabin. He watched a wren building a nest in a pile of brush beside the poultry yard as he puffed slowly on his clay pipe. He was dimly aware of the murmuring and quacking of the chickens and ducks that were picking about in the dirt and of the angry gobble of a turkey. Now and then he raised his eyes to gaze contentedly at the mountains surrounding his homeplace and the puffs of white clouds swirling about the distant peaks.

At Tsali's side, in a homemade chair, his plump old wife sat weaving a basket from oak splints. Beyond the clean-swept dooryard his second son, Ridge, was turning the rich, black earth of the garden plot with a plow drawn by an ox. Tsali's world seemed bathed in peace and contentment.

"This fine May weather is just right for making garden," Tsali remarked. "With our cow fresh and plenty of corn, beans, and squash, our gourds will surely be full through the coming moons."

"You're wrong." Tsali's wife flung back her long black braids and shivered as she spoke. "I constantly feel an evil wind. It keeps blowing over me and chilling my spirit with fear."

"Fear? There is nothing to fear, old woman. The Great Spirit has provided for us well in our hidden cove in the high hills. Our cabin of sawed planks is snug. We have sufficient ground to grow our food. Our sons are good. Our ox and cow and poultry are fat, and the forest about us is pleasant. Even now it fills our eyes with the beauty of the dogwood flowers. What more could a Cherokee wish?"

"The white man surrounds us," his wife complained. "Soon he will push us out. Night is falling on the Cherokee."

"You listen too much to your brother, Lowney, old woman. He has bent your ears with his tales. The white men are our friends. Have we not signed many treaties with them?"

His wife sighed deeply and bent over her work. "My brother says the white men's treaties are as false as the dawn that comes before true daylight. He says their roads all lead toward the setting sun. Lowney says that white soldiers are gathering to drive the Cherokee westward across the big river."

"That's foolish chatter, wife. Why should the white man wish to drive us westward? These mountains have been the home of the Cherokee since before the memory of the oldest of the old men, and our home shall remain here forever."

"The white man wants our land," Tsali's wife persisted. "With each treaty he has taken more. You have said that yourself."

"He does not want this rugged land." Tsali waved his arm about to include all of his hidden cove. "This steep mountain farm is of worth to no one but us."

"What of that dream you had?" his wife reminded. "It fills me with dread."

"I have many dreams. Which one, wife?"

"The one where all of your relatives met to talk and sing."

Tsali laughed. "Oh, that one. It was only a dream."

"Such a dream foretells death or banishment," his wife whispered fearfully. "You know it does. It was an omen. My brother says that we shall all be banished from our homes before another moon."

"This is the year of 1838, not some ancient time, and I am a civilized Cherokee," Tsali said proudly. "I do not believe in omens."

"You consulted the small magic stone, and it foretold your death." His wife stopped her weaving and looked up at Tsali with big, frightened eyes. "That was an omen, too."

"I do not believe in omens," Tsali repeated. "Hush your talk, old woman. I hear our youngest son coming. Maybe he has caught a fine trout for our supper. You will cook it and forget your fears and old-fashioned ideas."

Tsali waved to a young boy, dressed in deerskin trousers, with his black hair streaming behind him as he sped up the footpath toward the cabin. "Wasituni! Hail!"

"They're among us!" shouted the boy breathlessly as he reached the dooryard. "They're driving away our neighbors, even now!"

Ridge dropped the plow handles and sprinted across the yard to join the group. "Who? Who is driving away our neighbors?" he demanded. "You must be telling a tale, little brother."

"I saw them," Wasituni panted, dropping to the steps of the porch. "I saw the soldiers. As I was fishing in the deep pool we had dammed up in the stream, I heard shouting far below, in the cove where the Youngbirds live. I crept down through the laurel thicket, and I saw white soldiers, driving our neighbors before them, prodding them with the sharp points on the ends of their guns."

"Driving, Wasituni? Nobody drives a Cherokee!" Ridge's black eyes blazed, and he clenched his fists angrily. "I will go to their aid!"

Tsali laid a gnarled hand on Ridge's muscular arm. "Wait, my son. You would only bring them upon us more swiftly. Perhaps they will not find us here. Perhaps the soldiers will overlook this hidden, steep place. Many of our brothers, led by Utsala, have hidden themselves in the mountains high above the upper Oconaluftee River where no soldier can ever find them. If need be, we will join them there."

The mother dropped her basket, threw her apron over

her head, and sobbed. "They will find us," she cried. "I have told you we are doomed. My brother Lowney is right. Night is falling on the Cherokee. You knew it all the time, my husband, and you chose not to believe."

"How could I believe such a thing? It did not seem possible. Could Andrew Jackson have been speaking with a forked tongue when Chief Junaluska saved his life at the Battle of The Horseshoe? Jackson vowed, 'As long as the sun shines and the grass grows, there shall be friendship between us, and the feet of the Cherokee shall be pointed toward the East.' Would that Junaluska had let him die that day." Tsali bowed his head, and the tears rolled down his furrowed cheeks. "I weep for our people who have been betrayed, who are even now being driven from these mountains at Jackson's command." Then he threw up his head in a proud gesture. "But we shall never leave them. Never!"

As he spoke, his eldest son with his wife and three small children dashed into the clearing, followed by Lowney and his family, speeding as if pursued by an enemy.

"Quick! We must hide!" Lowney cried. "The soldiers are almost upon us. They are driving all of the Cherokee before them to a stockade at Bushnell!"

"Pretend to submit." Tsali had scarcely given the order when three soldiers of the United States Army strode into the yard, rattling their guns and barking orders.

The Indians gathered up what they could carry, and they all meekly started down the trail with the soldiers. Now and then they looked back to see the thieves who had followed the guards driving off their stock and looting the farmstead. Tsali's wife wept for her homely possessions—

her spinning wheel, her loom, her baskets and pots—but Wasituni and the men stepped along firmly, their heads held high.

As he trudged down the winding trail, they talked to each other in Cherokee, which the guards could not understand, and Tsali gave them all detailed instructions. "At the turn in the footpath," he said, "we will strike, but there must be no bloodshed."

At that moment a soldier prodded Tsali's wife with his bayonet to hurry her along, and the old man wanted to strike him, but restrained himself. As they rounded the turn, however, the men jumped upon the soldiers, snatching their rifles from them, while the women and children vanished into the forest. In the struggle a gun went off, killing a soldier, and the other two fled in panic. The Indian men and Wasituni joined the women, and they all started out for the upper peaks.

Tsali and his party traveled swiftly over familiar paths until they reached a hidden cave high up on what is now Clingman's Dome. There, with fellow exiles, they existed for a while on roots, berries, and whatever they could find to sustain life. Sometimes they could hear soldiers beating through the undergrowth below them, searching for escapees. Although they were near starvation in their hideout, not a Cherokee showed himself.

Finally, toward the end of the second moon, Old Tsali had a visitor. On watch that day, at the mouth of the cave, he saw a white man approaching up the secret way, but he did not hide.

"Our friend, Will-Usdi, comes," Tsali called to his comrades, and to the visitor he cried, "Welcome, Will-Usdi, Son of Yonaguska. I take you by the arm."

William Thomas, known as Will-Usdi (Little Will), was the trusted and beloved friend of all Cherokee and the adopted son of their Peace Chief, Yonaguska. He spoke sadly:

"I come with a heavy heart, my brother Tsali. I bring a message from General Winfield Scott, who commands the removal of the Cherokee to the West. He is but the servant of the President of the United States, who decrees this wicked thing. The message comes to you from the general, through your chief in hiding, Utsala. He consented for me to bring it to you. I, only, of all white men, know your hiding-place, and I would rather die than betray it. I come alone."

"Speak, my brother."

"General Scott says that if the persons responsible for the murder, as he calls it, of one of his soldiers will give themselves up for punishment, he will call off the troops he has combing the mountains for the Cherokee who are in hiding. He knows that even the seven thousand soldiers he has sent to hunt down every Cherokee man, woman and child, like animals in their dens, can never find them all, and he is tiring of the chase."

"Speak on, Will-Usdi."

"Now the general has guaranteed that those in hiding may remain in their mountains if the guilty ones will give themselves up at the fort at Bushnell. I do not urge you to go, my brother Tsali, but if you do, I mean to see that the promise is kept, even if I die in the process." Thomas raised his arms toward the sky, then pounded his fists together. "He shall keep that promise!"

Old Tsali drew himself up to the full height of his short stature. "We will go," he said.

True to his word, Tsali, his sons, and his brother-in-law followed their friend, Will Thomas, and after weary days and nights of traveling reached the stockade at Bushnell.

"We have come," Tsali told General Scott. When the commander ordered their immediate execution, they lined themselves up against trees, pushing off the blindfolds the soldiers had placed over their faces. "We are ready," Tsali said.

"Wait!" ordered General Scott, as he looked over the condemned men. "Why, one of these Indians is only a young lad. We do not shoot children."

Wasituni was saved, but Tsali, his two older sons, and his brother-in-law fell before the firing squad. Thus they saved more than a thousand of their fellow Cherokees from being hunted out of their hiding-places and driven into exile with the sixteen thousand others of their tribe.

The shameful removal of a whole tribe of people from their ancestral mountain homes to the arid, flat land beyond the Mississippi is one of the blackest chapters in the history of the United States. It was started during the presidency of Andrew Jackson (1829-37) and completed under the administration of Martin Van Buren (1837-41). Such statesmen as Daniel Webster and David Crockett and many others bitterly protested the inhumanity of the act. The hardships of that tragic emigration resulted in the deaths of thousands of Cherokee men, women, and children. The whole episode left a blot upon the history of our country that can never be erased.

Although the waters of Fontana Lake now cover the site of Fort Bushnell and the burial places of Old Tsali, his sons, and his brother-in-law, their heroic action lives on.

The story of the terrible journey of the "Trail of Tears" is the main theme of an outdoor drama by Kermit Hunter. This play, called *Unto These Hills,* can be seen each summer at the Mountainside Theatre near Cherokee and the heart of the Smoky Mountain National Park. Here still dwell the Eastern Cherokee, descendants of the Cherokee hero who saved his brethren from exile.

LIFE OF A POET

WHEN GEORGE MOSES HORTON BEGAN TO WRITE POEMS AT THE age of fourteen, he did not know that one day he would make his living from them. When we come to think of it, only rarely has any man made his living from poetry. In George Moses Horton's day, no North Carolinian had done so. Yet, even more unusual than Horton's profession is the fact of his making up poems at all. For, believe it or not, his first book was published before he had learned to write. Nor, at the time, could he read very easily.

Horton was born a slave on his master's plantation in Northampton County near the Roanoke River, not far from the Virginia state line. As a tiny tot, he sang little songs while following his mother down the tobacco rows as she worked.

He never went to school. It was only when his master moved to a farm eight miles south of Chapel Hill that his

self-education began. He found an old school book and
began to make out the letters in it. From a Bible and a
hymnbook of his mother's, he put the letters into words
so that they made some sense. He loved words because they
were so beautiful. Then, as he drove the cows to and from
the pasture, he fitted the words into songs. One Sunday,
much to his surprise, he discovered that he had "written"
a poem in his head. It started this way:

> Rise up, my soul, and let us go
>   Up to the gospel feast;
> Gird on the garment white as snow,
>   To join and be a guest.

This poem, of course, was like the hymns he had heard in
the country church he attended with his mother, brother,
sisters, and his master's big family. Yet, because he was
afraid his master would disapprove of a slave boy's making
up poems when he ought to be attending to his farm chores,
George Moses said nothing to anybody about his secret
occupation. But he kept repeating the lines aloud when he
was alone and added new poems from time to time.

Then something happened to change his life. Master
James Horton began to send him to Chapel Hill on Sundays
to sell fruits and vegetables raised on the farm. George
Moses' principal customers were the students attending the
University of North Carolina, which was located in the
village. Before they would buy, however, they insisted
that some trick be performed by the tall, handsome, dark-
skinned, twenty-year-old slave. George Moses knew only
one trick, which was to recite a poem. And this he did.
The students were amazed, for they liked poems very much.

When they asked him who wrote it, he replied that he himself had done it.

Furthermore, he explained that he would speak a poem on any subject they suggested. One lovesick student wanted a poem to send to his girl who lived far away. With hardly a pause, George Moses made up a verse on the spot. The student was so delighted that the slave was asked to repeat the lines while he copied them down, for they were far better than he could write himself. For this poem, the student gave George Moses 25 cents.

Soon the University young gentlemen ordered poems to be composed and brought in on the following Sunday. What they liked best were acrostics: poems in which the first letter in each line spelled out a girl's name. This was harder to do, but as he toiled in the fields during the week at the Horton farm, George Moses worked out the lines. Then on the next Sunday, with fruit in his basket and poems in his head, he returned to Chapel Hill and recited his poem as the student who had ordered it copied it down. Suppose the girl's name was Julia Shepard. George Moses was ready with this:

> Joy, like the morning, breaks from one divine—
> Unveiling stream which cannot fail to shine.
> Long have I strove to magnify her name
> Imperial, floating on the breeze of fame.
> Attracting beauty must delight afford. . . .

It was not long before George Moses came to the attention of important persons. His poems were printed in the newspapers, with an explanation that they were composed by a slave who could not even write. What a strange man,

everyone thought. Anyone as smart as George Moses Horton should not, certainly, be a slave. At Chapel Hill, a professor's wife began to teach him to write. Even the Governor of North Carolina tried to think of some way to set
him free. A fund was started to "buy" him from Master
James Horton and to send him away from a slave state
like North Carolina.

To add to the fund, some friends got together a number
of his poems and put them into a book. It was entitled *The
Hope of Liberty* and was published in Raleigh in 1829. Poet
Horton composed for his first volume several poems on his
disgraceful condition. Here is one verse:

> Must I dwell in Slavery's night
> And all pleasure take its flight
> Far beyond my feeble sight
>   Forever?

But the sales from the book, plus the money in the fund,
did not meet the high price Master James Horton demanded.
George Moses decided that, if he could not be legally set
free, he could at least free himself for work on his poetry.
Students were still eager to buy his love poems at 25 cents
and 50 cents apiece, and he could make some extra money
working around the college campus. So he proposed to his
master to "hire out his time"; that is, he would pay Master
Horton $3.00 a week not to have to work on the farm. This
is exactly what he did for many, many years. And so it was
that Horton not only made a living from his poetry but paid
his master for the privilege of doing so. Another book appeared.

Horton was an old man when the Civil War ended, and

he found himself free at last. When the Federal soldiers came to Chapel Hill, the former slave found a northern captain who took a liking to him at once. The captain liked poetry too and was as surprised as the University students had once been to discover that a Negro farm worker could write it. So Horton went along with the captain from place to place, writing love poems for the captain's Yankee soldiers and being paid for them. The captain was so pleased with Horton that he got a Raleigh printer to bring out a third book of the poems in 1865 called *Naked Genius*.

Free at last to go where he wanted, Poet Horton went north to Philadelphia and continued to support himself, at least in part, from his writing. By this time, he could use a pen rather well, and it was no longer necessary for someone to copy down the words as he spoke them. In Philadelphia, he made more money from stories in Sunday School pamphlets than he did from poems. Meanwhile, his friends in the South did not forget him, and when they were in Philadelphia they went to see him. He was a very old man when he died.

Today, when graceful lines of poetry seldom are paid for with money, George Moses Horton is remembered as one who made a living from his beautiful words.

RUNAWAY APPRENTICE

IN 1808 CASSO'S INN, ACROSS THE STREET FROM THE STATE HOUSE, was the most popular gathering place in the small capital city of Raleigh. It was favored because of its genial host, its fine accommodations for guests and horses, and especially for its esteemed serving couple, Jacob and Polly Johnson.

Although not a member of the gentry, Jacob Johnson was the most popular man in the City of Oaks. He was honest, good-natured, friendly to everyone, a fine hunter and fisherman, and a good companion to rich and poor. He often accompanied his wealthy friends on hunting and fishing trips in the neighboring countryside.

Jacob might have bettered his station in life, with his many connections, but he had no such ambition. He lived in a cottage behind the inn in the middle of the town where the most exciting happenings were always taking place. He had a good job. He was sexton of the Presbyterian Church and had the privilege of ringing the only bell in the city for services, weddings, and funerals. He had the friendship of everybody. Jacob was quite content with his lot, and so was his wife Polly.

Christmas week of 1808 had been especially merry at Casso's, ending with a grand ball over which pretty Peggy Casso presided as the belle of the town. There was jubilation in the snug, two-room cottage behind the inn on December 29 too, for Jacob and Polly Johnson had just that evening welcomed into the world their second son.

When Peggy Casso heard the news, she slipped away from the ball and ran up the stairs to the second-floor room of the Johnson's cottage.

"Oh, what a darling baby!" Peggy cried, as Polly Johnson folded back the blankets to show off her new little black-haired son. "What have you named him?"

"We haven't a name for a boy," Polly replied. "We expected a girl this time. You suggest a name, Mistress Peggy."

"Hm-m-m, let me think." Peggy screwed up her face in thought and leaned her rosy cheek against her hand. "Now, let's see. John? No, that's too plain for such a pretty baby. Robert? He's far too handsome for Robert. I know! Andrew! Andrew Jackson. Andrew Jackson Johnson. That's a fine-sounding name for a fine-looking baby."

"Andrew. Andrew Jackson. Andrew Jackson Johnson," murmured Polly, as if tasting the words. "Andrew, Andy. Why, it is a good name. What do you say, Jacob?"

"I say it's a fine name for a fine boy," replied Jacob. "Andy Johnson sounds just right to me."

So, Andrew Johnson the new baby was named, and before long the proud Jacob began taking little Andy about with him as he did the older son, William. The Johnsons' outings in the fields and woods, and their excursions to the infrequent circuses that showed in the small city of Raleigh, did not continue long, however, for the well-loved Jacob lost his life in saving a friend from drowning when little Andy was just three years old.

Polly set herself up in the weaving business in an effort to support herself and her two boys, but she had such a hard time that she found it necessary to bind the boys out as apprentice tailors to a man named James J. Selby.

Andy, now fourteen, was wiry, short of stature, and had black hair and snapping black eyes. He was a leader among the boys of the town. He loved to hunt and fish and roam the woods, as had his father, and all the other boys followed his lead, although he was said to be a "wild, harum-scarum boy, but with no unhonorable traits." He worked hard as an apprentice and was always agreeable and helpful to customers. It was at Selby's that he got his first taste of education.

There were no free schools in Raleigh in 1808, and Andy Johnson, whose mother could not read or write, had had no one to teach him his A B C's. But the foreman of the tailor shop helped give him a start, and a Dr. Hill often stopped in to read aloud to the bound boys as they sat cross-legged on the floor, sewing, or pressed finished garments with the big, hot iron called a tailor's goose.

Dr. Hill, an excellent reader, so inspired Andy that he resolved to learn to "speak slow," as the book admonished, and he practiced diligently, thus beginning the training in oratory that later served him well. He was so fascinated with the book of speeches that the good Dr. Hill gave it to him, and he tried with all his might to learn it by heart.

After two years as a bound boy, Andy, his brother, and two other apprentices ran away. Just why, no one knows, but it has been said that Mr. Selby insulted and thrashed his apprentices. At any rate, the tailor inserted an advertisement in the *Raleigh Gazette* of June 24, 1824, offering a ten-dollar reward for the return of "Andrew Johnson alone." Ten dollars was a large sum in 1824.

Andy and his brother tried working in several places, but, finding little to do, they made their way back home after two years. Andy went to Selby to apologize, but the tailor would not take him back, and he threatened to have the law on him. Nobody else would hire a runaway apprentice. Finally, the whole family—Mrs. Johnson had married again—loaded a two-wheeled cart with their few poor possessions and set out for Tennessee. Through the Piedmont, over the hills, across the mountains, and into the valleys they took turns, two by two, riding in the cart and walking. This was a common method of travel at that time for people who could not afford transportation for all.

At last the four of them reached Greeneville, Tennessee, where Andy immediately made many friends and secured work in a tailor shop. In March, 1827, when he was just nineteen years old, the future President of the United States set up a shop of his own.

Andy Johnson was a proud young man the day he showed his mother his own shop and read to her the sign swinging over the door of the small building, "A. Johnson, Tailor." He was still more proud the day he introduced her to Eliza McCardle, his new wife. She was a bonny Scottish girl, and she taught him to read better, to write, and to cipher.

Now, with a good business, a smart wife, and a host of friends, Andrew was ready to set out on his long career as a champion of the working class and a defender of the Constitution, with a fierce regard for truth and honesty. He was twice elected Governor of Tennessee, was a Senator in the United States Congress, was Vice-President under Abraham Lincoln, and became President of the United States when Lincoln was assassinated. The bound boy who had grown up in Raleigh, not even knowing how to write, had attained the highest office in the land.

In spite of violent criticism, fierce opposition, and even the threat of impeachment, Andrew Johnson stood steadfast in defense of the Constitution of the United States. At a time when the land was in chaos following the Civil War, he saved the country from further slander and bloodshed.

In Pullen Park, in Raleigh, there stands in memory of his greatness the restored small cottage where Andy Johnson first opened his black eyes. In the same city, on Capitol Square, there is a magnificent bronze monument to Andrew Johnson, Andrew Jackson, and James K. Polk—"Three Presidents North Carolina Gave the Nation."

LOUISA
AND THE STATE SONG

LOUISA TAYLOR WAS THIRTEEN YEARS OLD. SINCE HER FATHER'S death, she had helped her mother run the boarding house in Raleigh. She was glad to do it, because she needed money to pay for her piano lessons.

Louisa loved music, and often she would pick out on the piano a tune she had heard someone sing. Her music teacher, Mrs. Lucas, had praised her for this. When not in the kitchen or dining room, Louisa would usually be found sitting at the piano trying hard to improve her playing.

Mrs. Taylor was proud of her daughter. After dinner, she stood in the sitting-room doorway while Louisa played for the men who boarded there. One of the men who listened with particular attention was Louisa's great-uncle, Judge William Gaston.

Judge Gaston was a lonely old man from New Bern. He lived in Raleigh most of the time, for he was a justice of the Supreme Court. He ate his meals at Mrs. Taylor's house, just a block from Capitol Square, and lived next door in a tiny one-room office. At meal time, he would walk across the lawn, eat his meal, and then listen to Louisa play the piano. Later he would go back to work.

One evening, a group of singers and bell-ringers came to Raleigh. Louisa asked her mother if she might go to hear them. Mrs. Taylor was glad to tell her that it was all right, for she knew how Louisa loved music. Of all the music Louisa heard that night, one piece she liked the most. It was sung by four brothers. At the end of each stanza, they shouted, "Hurrah! Hurrah!"

As she walked home, she could not get the music out of her head. On the street she heard other people humming it also. The next morning she jumped from her bed, helped her mother in the dining room, then went straight to the sitting room to pick out the music on the piano. Some people say she went out and found the Swiss singers and got the music from them. Soon she could play it well. She liked it so much that she played it more often than any other piece.

Once, as Mrs. Taylor and Judge Gaston listened to Louisa playing the tune, Mrs. Taylor said, "Uncle, that piece would make a beautiful song, maybe one for our state of North Carolina."

"Do you really think so?" asked the Judge.

"Other states have their own songs, but here in North Carolina we do not. Uncle, you have written poems in the past. Now, won't you write some words for this music so that we can all sing them?"

"I like the tune, and I will see what I can do," said the judge.

Judge Gaston stepped across the lawn to his office. Louisa's tune was ringing in his mind. Soon he had written out a few lines. They went like this:

Carolina! Carolina! Heaven's blessings attend her!
While we live we will cherish, protect, and defend her!

He wrote a few more lines. And then he came to the end of the first verse. Here he wrote the chorus:

Hurrah! Hurrah! the Old North State forever!
Hurrah! Hurrah! the good Old North State!

Judge Gaston took his first verse and walked over to the house, where Louisa was still playing.

"Let's see if these words fit," he said.

Louisa played the music softly, and Judge Gaston hummed along. He took out a word here, changed a word there. He wanted his words to fit the music perfectly. When he was satisfied, he went back to his office and wrote a second verse telling about North Carolina's fight for liberty. He brought the second verse to Louisa and tried it out as before. There was a third verse about the good men of North Carolina, a fourth about the fine women, and, at last, verse number five. Louisa kept playing the music for him.

The next morning, he brought a piece of paper to his niece, Mrs. Taylor, and said, "Well, Eliza, here is your song." Louisa stood by, proud of her part in making this song. At breakfast, with the boarders all around the table, Judge Gaston read the words aloud, and the boarders applauded.

Some time later, Louisa played and sang the song for

Mrs. Mary Lucas, her music teacher. Mrs. Lucas was very pleased. After Louisa had learned the words by heart, she taught them to a friend of hers. One evening, Louisa and her friend sang the song to the boarders. It was the first time our state song was ever sung for an admiring audience.

Five years passed, and Louisa had grown into a beautiful young woman, eighteen years old. There was much excitement in Raleigh, for a big meeting was being held. Thousands of people came to the city for the great Whig convention. The Whigs were a political party, like the Democrats and Republicans today.

The big meeting was held among the trees of Capitol Square. A platform for the speakers was built so that they could be seen and heard by the thousands standing and sitting on the grass. As soon as one speaker stopped, another one started. Mrs. Mary Lucas, Louisa's music teacher, was asked to provide music between the long speeches, so she asked fifty young women to sing and play guitars. Another platform was built for them just below the speakers' platform.

On the second day of the big meeting—Tuesday, October 6, 1840—the ladies got to their feet when one of the speakers had just stopped. The crowd was moving about on the grass among the trees.

Then the ladies began to sing: "Carolina! Carolina! Heaven's blessings attend her!" It was Judge Gaston's song that they had learned. They sang the first verse, then the second. By the time they got to the third, all the people shouted the chorus with them: "Hurrah! Hurrah! the Old North State forever!" When the five verses were finished, the crowd still shouted the words: "The good Old North State!"

Was Louisa one of the fifty young women? We do not know. But when she heard how all good North Carolinians liked the song she had helped Judge Gaston write, we can be sure she was a very proud young lady.

In 1927, Judge Gaston's song was made the official state song of North Carolina, just as "The Star-Spangled Banner" is the song of the United States of America.

In New Bern today, we can visit the home of Judge Gaston and the little law office he used when not in Raleigh. Gaston County and the city of Gastonia are named for him.

DR. MITCHELL'S MOUNTAIN

IT WAS EARLY AFTERNOON ON SATURDAY, JUNE 27, 1857. DR. Elisha Mitchell was talking with his son Charles outside a crude shelter they called Mountain House. Just behind them were the high ridges and peaks of the Black Mountains, over which Dr. Mitchell had climbed several times.

"Now, Charles," he said, "you go on back to the hotel by the river bank. Your sister will need your cheerful company."

"Are you sure you'll be all right?" Charles had only recently graduated from the University of North Carolina, where his father was professor of mathematics. Dr. Mitchell was sixty-four years old and ought not, thought Charles, to be mountain-climbing without someone along.

"Yes, of course."

Dr. Mitchell was a large man, weighing over two hundred pounds. In spite of his age, he was still healthy and full of vigor. He went on talking.

"I want to find that balsam tree where I measured the height of that tallest mountain years ago. Then I plan to go down the other side of the ridge to visit Big Tom Wilson, the bear hunter who was with me at the time. You come back here to Mountain House on Monday to meet me. Now, go ahead and stay with your sister. She will be lonesome."

Charles hesitated. He didn't want to leave his father. He knew that Dr. Mitchell had been tramping these high mountains in western North Carolina for thirty years, but he was worried anyway.

Yet Charles knew, too, how important it was that his father find that balsam tree and measure again that particular high peak. On the basis of his first measurement, Dr. Mitchell had stated that his mathematical instruments proved that this particular mountain in the Blacks was the highest point of land east of the Mississippi. Mt. Washington in New Hampshire had been considered the highest up to the time Dr. Mitchell had stood by the balsam tree.

Mountain people, like Big Tom Wilson, loved Dr. Mitchell for the acclaim he had brought to their beautiful country. They loved him, too, because he was a gentle man who did not put on airs or boast of his discovery. They were troubled when other men wrote that they doubted that Dr. Mitchell had measured correctly; and one rascal said he didn't believe for a minute that Dr. Mitchell had ever climbed the very mountain he claimed was the highest one of all.

So, when classes at Chapel Hill had been dismissed for

summer vacation, Dr. Mitchell, with his son and his daughter, headed towards the Blacks. He was determined to take the measurement again from the balsam tree.

Dr. Mitchell was a strong-minded man, and as Charles faced him just then, he knew he would do exactly as his father ordered.

"Very well," he sighed, "I'll meet you here on Monday."

The vigorous professor turned and started up the steep slope. The mountain laurel and rhododendron were flaming with color in those late June days. White, pink, and purple blossoms sometimes hid the green leaves. Charles watched the retreating figure of his father as he climbed carefully among the rocks. Some of the stones were just the right size for building rock walls like the ones in Chapel Hill. It was Dr. Mitchell, born in Connecticut, who had brought to the university village the notion of putting up rock walls instead of fences. It was a New England custom.

Charles stood there gazing after his father. Dr. Mitchell, now high above him, turned around and waved. A moment later he had disappeared among the flowers and the dark green mountain trees.

It was the last moment Charles, or anyone else, ever saw him alive.

For two days, time and time again, the sight of his father, standing there waving, came back to Charles. On Monday he left his sister at the hotel and hiked to Mountain House. When his father did not return, he was deeply troubled. Dr. Mitchell was not there on Tuesday either, and the young man could bear it no longer. The next day, he sought out a bear hunter named John Stepp, who knew how to find his way even where there were no trails in the mountains; and the two of them headed for Big Tom Wilson's house across the high ridge.

On Thursday they sighted Big Tom in his yard. A tall, strong, rangy man now in his thirties, Big Tom had the keen, pale, gray eyes of the mountain people. He was already noted as one of the best bear hunters of the region. The two men rushed toward him with their question.

Big Tom was puzzled. "Dr. Mitchell? No, I haven't seen him. How long has it been since he left Mountain House?"

"Five days," said Charles. His very worst fears seemed to be confirmed.

"We'll find him. But it will take till tomorrow to get all the men we'll need. I'll send out word right now."

The next day was Friday. When the news came to them that Dr. Mitchell was lost, mountain men dropped whatever they were doing and came to Big Tom's house. They were known as the Men of Yancey County. Across the ridge, the news also had gone out, and the Men of Buncombe County were gathering. That very morning a double assault was made against the highest mountain east of the Mississippi River to find the man who had first established its height. Dozens of seekers scattered across the steep wilderness.

On Saturday a cold and steady rain drenched the searchers. But even more mountain men came to look for the professor they honored. Soon the number of climbers reached a hundred. On Sunday, a dense fog settled upon the mountains. They had found no clue, no footprint. They were tired and hungry.

Zeb Vance, later Governor of North Carolina during the Civil War, was among those who looked behind every boulder and into every cave. He saw a fat heifer grazing nearby. "Kill it," he said, "and blow the hunting horn." When the men came over the cliffs, they cut huge chunks from the heifer and roasted them over a fire. Some of the searchers were so famished that they gulped down raw pieces of the beef.

By Tuesday, Big Tom Wilson's group decided to make their way down the Yancey County side of the mountain. The Men of Buncombe would continue to cover the southern slope of the range. Suddenly one of Big Tom's men shouted that he had found a footprint in a soft mossy spot, but he could not be sure it was Dr. Mitchell's. Perhaps it was only the imprint of a bear's paw.

Big Tom leaned over the moss. "No," he said, "this was made by no bear. Dr. Mitchell has been here—many days ago. A bear will go along the rocks, where he leaves no scent of his trail. Only a man picks soft mossy ground to step on."

Big Tom was excited. Everyone was. At last, there was a clue! Down the mountain side, Big Tom pointed to a laurel bush. "Look at that," he cried. "Somebody has turned those laurel leaves upside down. See how the light underside of the leaves is turned up, and the dark upper side turned down. And five feet from the ground! You can bet your life it was no bear, either. Bears don't walk on their hind legs and turn laurel leaves upside down."

Then, for a while, the trail was lost. But not for long. Farther on, Big Tom found a rotten balsam tree, which once had fallen and lay caught in a rhododendron thicket. Big Tom noticed that the trunk of the decayed tree had recently been broken. "This was broken by a man," he explained. "Only men and bears ever get up this high on the mountain. If a bear had come by here, he would have slipped by under the trunk. But a man, seeing the tree was rotten, would put his foot on it, break it, and go on."

Just beyond, Big Tom Wilson and his party stopped. They had reached a clearing in the woods and could see out into the valley. Six miles away, now that the sun was shining again, was a clear view of Big Tom's house. It was Tuesday, July 7—ten days since Charles Mitchell had last seen his father.

Big Tom stood in the clearing, thinking. It was all so simple. He realized now what had happened. Ten days ago, with evening coming on, Dr. Mitchell had stood in that very clearing and seen the house in the valley. Then Dr. Mitchell had made a foolish decision. Instead of camping on the mountain and pushing on to Big Tom's the next morning, he had made up his mind to get to Big Tom's that night.

Dr. Mitchell's trail was easy to follow now. Big Tom could see exactly what Dr. Mitchell had done. He was hurrying to reach the valley before dark. No longer was there the careful footprint in the moss. Now a bush showed how the professor had run against it. Then there was a rock with a harsh streak across it, proving Dr. Mitchell had slid down it. Big Tom's ears picked up the sound of a rushing mountain stream. So the professor had decided to walk down the stream to the valley! Walking the stream bed would keep him from getting lost. Yes, here was the very spot he had entered the icy water, a gash in the bank. Dr. Mitchell had waded down the stream, up to his waist in deep places.

Big Tom directed his men to watch on both sides of

the creek. They would discover where Dr. Mitchell had got back onto the bank. But there was no sign. Gradually Big Tom was aware of a soft, plunging sound of water. As he descended the stream, it became louder—and then very loud indeed. There was a waterfall below them. When Dr. Mitchell came along this way, it must have been dark. Why didn't the old explorer stop and stay the night? Big Tom's mind was whirling. He could imagine Dr. Mitchell rushing ahead, running onto the slippery rocks.

And then, there in front of Big Tom and his Men of Yancey was the waterfall, racing forty feet straight down into a deep pool. Yes, and there was the long, descending gash in the topmost rock, just where the waterfall began.

Holding to a sturdy laurel branch, Big Tom leaned out over the rock and looked into the pool below. Even Big Tom had never, in all his bear hunts, been to this waterfall. He doubted that any man had ever seen it or had known it was there.

Big Tom held tight to the laurel, scanning the pool. His sharp eyes wandered along the cool bank of the pool. There, in a curve of the dark waters, he saw a hat floating —a hat that belonged to an old friend of his.

The search was over.

They found Dr. Mitchell's body seven feet below the surface, tangled in a rhododendron snag. His pack was with him—containing his few simple needs, plus the necessary mathematical instruments he had used to measure the highest mountain in all the eastern part of North America. There were a few coins in his pocket; his watch had stopped at 8:19.

Lovingly, the Men of Yancey wrapped the precious body

of their friend in stout sacking, attached it to a pole, then put each end of the pole on the shoulder of a man. The long climb began. Straight up to the top of Dr. Mitchell's mountain they would go, the men at the poles frequently taking turns. They would bury Dr. Mitchell on the very top of the mountain whose greatness and tallness he had discovered.

But Charles requested that his father be buried at Asheville, and so he was. A year later, the Men of Buncombe and the Men of Yancey met again and took Dr. Mitchell once more to the highest mountain in the East—6,684 feet above sea level.

Today a paved road leads almost to the top of Mt. Mitchell, as the peak is now named. His grave is there, and a high tower looks out over Yancey and Buncombe counties. Near Mt. Mitchell, and just a little less towering, is a pinnacle called Big Tom. The forest rangers at Mt. Mitchell point it out proudly. It was named for Big Tom Wilson, who had led in the search for Dr. Mitchell and who, in his lifetime, had killed one hundred and fourteen bears.

WE ARE CALLED
"TAR HEELS"

WHEN NORTH CAROLINIANS GET TOGETHER FOR A GOOD TIME, sooner or later they will probably start singing:

> I'm a Tar Heel born,
> I'm a Tar Heel bred,
> And when I die
> I'm a Tar Heel dead.

Nobody knows who wrote the music to this song, and nobody knows who wrote the words. As a matter of fact, nobody knows exactly how a North Carolinian came to be known as a Tar Heel. There are, however, many legends about its origin and even a few facts from history to support the legends. It all started in the early days of the colony of North Carolina when she still belonged to England— before she was a state in the United States of America.

As soon as the settlers had cleared a few acres of land, built their homes, and planted some crops, they looked around for possible ways to make money. Except for the sandbanks, the entire region along the coast was covered with a vast forest of pine trees. After a slit was made in the tall green pines, a thick liquid called raw turpentine oozed from the cut. The turpentine was later boiled and processed into rosin, tar, and pitch. These products, called naval stores, were used in shipbuilding.

Sent back to England, naval stores brought a good price. This was one of the few ways, besides selling his tobacco, that the North Carolina farmer had to make money. He needed ready cash to pay his taxes and to buy salt, coffee, and other household necessities. Furthermore, he found he could tap the pine trees at times when he was not busy planting and harvesting crops.

So much did North Carolinians have to do with naval stores that people in other states called them Tar Burners and Tar Boilers. These nicknames were meant to be a bit insulting. So were the nicknames given to the state itself, which was called the Turpentine State or the Tar and Turpentine State. Seldom did folks in North Carolina use these terms. For a nickname, they preferred the Old North State. This name, we remember, was used by Judge William Gaston when he wrote his song in 1835.

One thing is sure about naval stores: they are sticky. If

you put your hand into a barrel of tar, it will take a long time and hard work to get it clean again. When the poorer North Carolina farmer worked at boiling his turpentine, he had no shoes to wear. Soon the bottoms of his feet were covered with black tar, and he did not always bother to get the tar off. This was before the Civil War. According to legend—and we are not sure of this—someone would see the poor farmer and say, "Look at that tar heel."

Later, during the Civil War between the southern and northern states, this same North Carolina farmer became a soldier. He quit burning turpentine in the big pine forests and marched off to fight for his state. Sometimes he was so poor that he had no shoes to wear. Perhaps a bit of tar still stuck to his heels.

Legend accounts for a story in the early months of the war at the Battle of Bull Run in northern Virginia, near Washington, D.C. We are told that during the heat of the battle, a Confederate general was watching the troops. With pride, he remarked, "That regiment of North Carolinians must have tar on their heels to make them stick as they do."

History takes the place of legend in 1863 at a battle in Tennessee. Now, for sure, the North Carolina soldiers fighting for the Confederacy were called Tar Heels. They seemed to stick in the front lines and would not retreat when the battle raged around them. According to a newspaper reporter, the term was used "perhaps from their tenacity of purpose as well as their having been enlisted in the piney woods of the Old North State."

The following year, some South Carolinians met some North Carolina soldiers. As they passed each other, one of the South Carolina men yelled: "Go it, Tar Heels!"

"Yes, we are Tar Heels," a North Carolina trooper replied, *"and tar sticks."*

To make fun of his rivals, a South Carolina soldier shouted back. "Yes, and when the fire gets hot, the *tar runs.*"

North Carolina men were still ashamed to be called Tar Heels. The term made them think of how poor they were, not rich like the South Carolinians and Virginians of that period. But then—according to legend—something happened to change their minds about the words.

The most popular man in North Carolina during the years of the Civil War was the Governor of the state, Zebulon B. Vance. The citizens loved him, for he was a good, strong man with many a joke to tell. The soldiers loved him too, for he would leave his office in Raleigh and go to visit them right on the battlefields. Always he had something funny to say, as well as something inspiring.

Late in the war, he went all the way to northern Virginia to see his beloved North Carolina soldiers. Speaking to a group of them, he began: "I do not know how to address you boys. I can't say fellow citizens because none of us are citizens of this state of Virginia where we are now. I cannot say fellow soldiers because I am not one of you. Therefore, I have concluded to address you as fellow Tar Heels."

Shouts and yells of delight followed his words. Never again would North Carolinians be ashamed of their nickname. If their Governor took pride in calling himself a Tar Heel, so would each one of them.

The nickname *stuck*. Today every loyal North Caro-

linian wants to be known as a tried and true Tar Heel. His
heart swells "with gladness" whenever he sings:

> I'm a Tar Heel born,
> I'm a Tar Heel bred,
> And when I die
> I'm a Tar Heel dead.

DARK NIGHTS
AND HIGH TIDES

WHEN NORTH CAROLINA ADOPTED THE ORDINANCE OF SECESSION
on May 20, 1861, Governor John W. Ellis had already begun collecting supplies for the use of the Confederacy. He
realized that war was inevitable and had a force of soldiers
ready and a small, three-vessel navy. The Federals laughed
at the tiny North Carolina navy, calling it the Mosquito
Fleet.

In the earliest months of the Civil War both sides knew
that whoever controlled the coastline of North Carolina,
with its navigable inlets and harbors, would have the ad-
vantage. The leaders of the South also realized that, in
spite of bold raids by the Mosquito Fleet on Union shipping, the Confederacy must build forts to prevent the

enemy from taking over North Carolina ports. They must also somehow acquire ships that could bring in supplies from abroad. They needed guns, ammunition, material for uniforms, medical supplies, coffee, tea, salt, sugar, and other necessities. The South was woefully short of these and was forced to depend on outside help.

By early fall of 1861, four small forts had been built along the Outer Banks in addition to Fort Macon, which already guarded Beaufort Inlet. All of these forts were undermanned and underequipped, but they put up brave fights before they fell, one by one in 1861 and 1862, before the bombardments of the Union navy. This left the North Carolina coastline under the command of the Federals—or so they thought.

The Old North State still had one deep-water port open to her shipping, if it could be reached. Twenty miles up the Cape Fear River was the harbor of Wilmington, with a direct rail line to Richmond and the headquarters of the Confederate States and armies. Its access point was New Inlet. If ships could enter here, supplies could still be secured and distributed. Although the Federals set up an elaborate blockade from Alexandria, Virginia, to Florida, it failed to stop the supplies from reaching the Confederacy. Southerners hurried to construct Fort Fisher, "the Gibraltar of America," on Confederate Point as a guard for New Inlet. Equipped with men and powerful guns, it was put under the command of an energetic and daring officer, Colonel William Lamb.

The iron-hulled, wooden steamers of the Union Navy were slow and heavy, entirely unsuited to navigate shallows and shoals. They were often short of coal; their crews were bored and discontented with long stretches of sea-duty. They had no ready sources of supply, and they grew restless awaiting the provision ships. For repairs, the Union vessels must make long runs back to northern bases, which weakened their blockade system.

On the other hand, the Confederacy was able to secure from England and Scotland, countries sympathetic to the South, a large number of swift, easily managed side-wheel steamers. These light vessels were painted pale gray or buff, for camouflage, and were commanded by dedicated and clever European or southern captains. These blockade-runners, as they came to be called, were too small to ferry goods back and forth across the wide Atlantic. However, they were well able to take cargo to Bermuda, the Bahamas, and Nova Scotia, unload it, and reload with supplies for the South. England, France, and other countries shipped supplies to these ports so they could be taken on to the South. Blockade-runners were able to hide from the gunboats of the blockade more frequently than seemed possible, because the swift, small vessels could hug the shoreline and navigate shallow water in which the large Union warships dared not go.

Blockade-runners, with such names as *Thistle, Will-o-the-Wisp, Chameleon,* and *Phantom,* needed only the dark of the moon for leaving and returning to Wilmington and a high tide for crossing the bar. The deck hands and officers wore rope-soled shoes or went barefooted and always spoke in whispers. The boom of the surf usually concealed the sound of the paddle-wheels.

In the South, the women, children, loyal slaves, and old men left behind at home worked hard and long to keep their troops supplied with the necessities of life as well as arms and ammunition. It was also difficult to keep themselves clothed and fed. Soon the task grew impossible. Food and clothing became more and more scarce, and arms could not be had. The swift, silent vessels that regularly ran the blockade kept the Confederacy alive. They brought in more than three times the number of arms produced at home, desperately needed supplies of all kinds, and some luxuries. One runner, the *Banshee,* even brought in an Arabian horse as a gift from an agent in Egypt to President Jefferson Davis. It is said that the loud whinnying of the animal was heard by the crew of a Union gunboat. The gunboat gave chase and the *Banshee* barely escaped.

Some of the blockade-runners were owned by the Confederacy, but a larger number were owned by foreign or southern businessmen who were more interested in profit than in patriotism. Many kept their names a secret. They offered enormous wages, as much as four or five thousand dollars to a captain for one round trip. A deck hand could make two hundred and fifty dollars, always in gold, with a bonus at the end of a successful run. Often the captains did a side business on their own, and the sailors engaged in illegal trade.

England, especially, was desperate for cotton to keep her mills going and her mill workers from starvation. Since the South grew more cotton than anything else, the "white gold," as cotton was called, proved a perfect substitute for money for trading purposes. Tobacco was also used as currency to purchase the Enfield rifles, lead and saltpeter for making ammunition, blankets, boots, shoes, cloth for uniforms, and medical supplies for the army. Tobacco also purchased such mundane articles as toothbrushes, spools of thread, and calico for civilian use. Speculators bought cheap and sold high, and some reaped fortunes.

The long layovers in the Bahamas, Bermuda, and Nova Scotia gave the sailors, often foreigners, ample opportunity to spend their high wages and their profits from private ventures, and so they signed on for further runs. A lack of crew was never a problem for the blockade-runners, even though many of the ships were taken or sunk by the Federals.

All blockade-runner captains were not greedy for profit, however, and many sailed these ships for love of the South. One of the most able and daring who was utterly devoted to the Confederate cause was Captain John Wilkinson, skipper of the *Giraffe*. The *Giraffe* was a Scottish-built steamer that could make fourteen knots an hour, and Captain Wilkinson made many successful runs in her before he was captured. He was tried and released by the Federals, only to take up again as master of the *Robert E. Lee,* the most renowned of all the blockade-runners. Aboard the *Robert E. Lee,* Captain Wilkinson made twenty-one successful round trips in one year, although his ship was hit several times and he had many close escapes. He established for the Confederacy an effective signal system of flags by day and shaded lights by night. Several years after the war was over, he retired to his native Virginia and wrote a best-selling book called *Adventures of a Blockade-Runner.* It is from Captain John Wilkinson's memoirs that other authors have gathered much of their information about the sea war waged by the Confederacy along the North Carolina coast.

While blockade-runners were used mainly for transporting materials, they frequently carried human cargo. These people were refugees fleeing to Bermuda, deserters who stowed away among the piled-up bales of cotton, Confederate agents bound for missions abroad, and spies for the South.

Two of the frequent passengers on blockade-runners were famous Confederate woman spies: bold Belle Boyd, who was said to have eaten dispatches when in danger of capture; and the beauteous widow, Rebel Rose Greenhow. In September of 1864, Rebel Rose was returning from England on the *Condor* with important papers for President Jefferson Davis and a large amount of gold, when the ship was attacked by Union gunboats near New Inlet. She asked to be put into a boat to try to make shore, but unfortunately, the small boat capsized. Mrs. Greenhow was drowned, weighted down by the gold sewn about in her clothing. The next day her body washed ashore, and she was wrapped in a Confederate flag and buried in Wilmington with full military honors. A monument in that city marks her grave.

The captain of an unfortunate blockade-runner that was caught usually made an effort to burn or sink his vessel to avoid having his goods fall into the hands of the enemy. Sometimes this failed. It has been said that blockade-running was perhaps the most successful large-scale operation carried on by the South during the whole four years of the war.

The Port of Wilmington and Fort Fisher held out until near the end, when both fell to the Federals on January 15, 1865, bombarded simultaneously from land and sea. But before the fall of Wilmington, it had received at its wharfs about sixty-five million dollars worth of supplies, brought in by more than a hundred blockade-runners in some four hundred trips. These desperately needed supplies were then shipped over the Wilmington and Weldon Railroads, "the Lifeline of the South," to Richmond and other points.

It is fascinating to read the lists of cargo of some of the blockade-runners, such as that of the *Ella and Annie*. She left St. George, Bermuda, on August 17, 1863, loaded with such items as five hundred cases of Austrian rifles, hundreds of boxes of ammunition, nitric and muriatic acid, surgical instruments, saddles, and horseshoes—a cargo worth $180,000, all of which fell into the hands of the Federals.

Many another cargo, just as valuable, lies in the waters around and beyond New Inlet, either ruined by the elements or awaiting salvage after these hundred years by archaeologists and treasure-seekers. The site of Fort Fisher is preserved as a State Historical Site, with restoration of parts of its impressive earthen breastworks. There is also a visitors' center and museum with a large collection of Civil War relics from land and sea and a scale model of the fort itself. It can be visited daily by the public.

AT LUCY BENNETT'S
FARMHOUSE

FOR ALMOST FOUR YEARS, THE CONFEDERATES OF THE SOUTH AND
the Federals of the North had fought each other in a bitter
war. Not only North against South, but the war was also
Americans against Americans, cousins against cousins,
brothers against brothers.

By the beginning of 1865, in spite of everything the
southern soldiers could do, they began to realize that they
were going to lose. There were more people in the North,
more manufacturing plants, and more wealth. Southern
bravery alone could not win the war.

In a way, North Carolina had been lucky. Very few big
battles, like those in Tennessee and Virginia, had been
fought on her soil. She sent supplies to the Confederate
army, and she sent out more soldiers than any other state,
but the home folks remained fairly safe.

Then, early in 1865, General William Tecumseh Sherman, leading a force of sixty thousand Union soldiers, began sweeping up from the west and south, destroying cities, burning homes, and taking away all the farm animals. He came into North Carolina, sent part of Fayetteville up in flames, then pushed on eastward, stripping the countryside as he went. Sherman thought the only way to end the war quickly was to destroy the towns and farms of the enemy. Unfortunately for the South, he was right.

The only person who had
Sherman was General Joseph
a small army of tired Confe
the only fresh group was
Brigade, made up of boys ei§
The older North Carolina mei
these boys had been called ir
state.

At Bentonville, south of Smithfield, General Johnston decided he would try to put a halt to Sherman's march. He knew there was little possibility he could do so, but for two days, there at Bentonville, the Confederates fought the Union troops. It was no use. General Johnston finally had to give ground. The Battle of Bentonville was the last battle of the Civil War.

After resting his army at Goldsboro, Sherman and his men started towards Raleigh. When they entered the capital city, which surrendered without a fight, the streets were deserted, all doors and windows shut. Sherman's men fanned out from Raleigh, stripping the farms of every chicken, pig, and barrel of flour.

Johnston retreated westward toward Durham's Station

(as Durham was then called) and Hillsborough, avoiding a battle he could not hope to win. When he received the news from Virginia that General Robert E. Lee had surrendered, Johnston knew how foolish it was to continue the war. The entire South was now occupied by the Union soldiers—except for a small portion of central North Carolina. Johnston believed that he should not allow another soldier to be killed or wounded in a hopeless cause. On April 14 he sent a message to Sherman and suggested that the two have a talk. Sherman agreed to meet Johnston at a point half way between Durham's Station and Hillsborough.

On Easter Monday morning, April 17, 1865, Sherman left Durham's Station, now occupied by his men. In front of him was a soldier with a white flag, followed by a unit of cavalry. Then came General Sherman himself and his staff. The victorious general hardly looked like the conqueror he was. Forty-five years old, he was quite tall, with uncombed red hair. An old felt hat sat clumsily on his head and his unbuttoned blue army coat flapped with each step of his beautiful white horse. He looked more like a private than a general.

At about the same time, Johnston was leaving Hillsborough, also with a soldier carrying a white flag, followed by a cavalry unit. Johnston was fifty-eight, thirteen years older than Sherman. He was of slight build, but his gray beard was carefully groomed, and he wore his best gray Confederate uniform neatly buttoned to the chin.

Between Durham's Station and Hillsborough, the two white flags met. The two generals—the conquering one and the defeated one—saw each other for the first time in their lives. Both generals had attended West Point. Both had fought early in the war at Bull Run, and they had opposed their armies in that last battle of the war at Bentonville. But this was the first time they had met. They shook hands before dismounting from their horses.

The two generals looked about for a quiet place to talk. Nearby was the farmhouse of Lucy Bennett, who was at home with her four children. It was a small house, with a stone chimney, only one room downstairs, and an attic overhead. Inside were several chairs, a bed, a table, and a desk. After Lucy Bennett agreed to let the two generals use her house, she took her four children and retired to one of her farm buildings.

It was about noon when the two generals went into the house and closed the door. Right away, Johnston told Sherman that he realized it was folly to keep fighting, that he wanted to surrender all the remaining armies of the Confederacy on the same terms General Robert E. Lee had been given a week before. Johnston wanted to end the war once and for all, not merely the military part of it. Sherman was undecided as to what he should do. They talked on as the afternoon advanced.

Meanwhile, outside the Bennett farmhouse, soldiers from the South and the North, who only a month ago had been fighting each other to the death, became very friendly. There, under the oak trees, they leaned against the farm sheds and told of their war experiences. The men in the blue and the men in the gray swapped horses, ran races to pass the time away, and spoke of the future when war would be no more. There was no bitterness. They were Americans all. A casual onlooker would never have believed that only a short while ago these men had been enemies.

Finally, Sherman told Johnston he would meet him again the following day. Thus, on Tuesday they sat once more in Mrs. Bennett's farmhouse. Sherman wrote out the terms, and Johnston agreed to them with relief. State governments in the South were to be recognized, and political rights and property rights were to be restored. In other words, the South was not to be punished by the victorious North. Yet Sherman made clear to Johnston that the surrender terms were not final. They had to be approved in Washington.

As the generals went their separate ways, the soldiers from both sides believed that the war was now over. From the grounds of the Bennett place, they gathered leaves and spring flowers as souvenirs to take with them as keepsakes of the historic occasion.

Some days later, Sherman was informed that the government in Washington had not approved the political part of the surrender terms. The unhappy Sherman was instructed to sign only a military truce.

For a third time, on April 26, the two generals met at Lucy Bennett's farmhouse. Now that the war was soon to be over, Sherman wished to be as kind as possible to the South. He was, in fact, quite angry that the North had not approved the liberal terms he had offered Johnston, and he apologized to Johnston for the necessity of a new surrender. Under the circumstances he outlined the very best terms he could. The Confederate soldiers were to keep their private property, their side arms, and their horses. The horses would be needed to plant crops when they got home.

Also, the Federals were to give each Confederate soldier rations for ten days, with wagons to haul them. Sadly Johnston signed the papers, and the war was finally at an end.

The two generals, now friends, shook hands and said good-bye. The Confederate soldiers were mustered out at Greensboro, and Sherman's army soon was marching towards Washington, D.C., for a victory parade.

In the years that followed, Johnston and Sherman remained good friends. Often they wrote to each other about the three meetings at Lucy Bennett's farmhouse where they had ended the terrible Civil War between the South and the North. Sherman was a good friend, too, of all the southern people, who came to understand that his destructive campaign was planned to end the war, not to show hatred of his fellow Americans.

When Sherman died in 1891, Johnston stood bare-headed at his funeral, at which he was an honorary pallbearer. From this exposure in the cold February air, General Johnston became ill and died the following month.

Today, Lucy Bennett's farmhouse and outbuildings have been restored to look just as they did in April, 1865. Exactly one hundred years later, in April, 1965, Hubert H. Humphrey, the Vice-President of the United States, dedicated the site where the two generals had brought an end to the war between the Americans of the North and the Americans of the South. Many North Carolinians now visit the Bennett place, which is open to the public.

"THAR SHE BLOWS"

CHARLEY JOE SHIVERED AND TURNED UP THE COLLAR OF HIS
pea jacket, as he slogged over the sand dunes toward the boat
landing opposite Diamond City. "Here it is May, and cold
enough to freeze a porpoise's snout," he muttered to himself. "Well I'll be! If Cap'n Willy isn't still at it!" He hurried toward a gale-twisted live oak that was the tallest tree
on Lookout Hill.

"Ahoy there, Cap'n Willy!" Charley Joe hailed the old
man who was climbing hand over hand up the boards
nailed to the trunk of the oak. Cap'n Willy was bundled
to the ears with a red scarf showing between his oilskins
and sou'wester. "Season ended yesterday, Cap'n," the boy
called. "No need to be sighting for whales this blustery
morning."

"Get on with ye, lad," the old man called down good-
naturedly from the height of the crude shelter built in the
tree for the whale-spotters. "It's my job to look out for
whales and I don't aim to stop, season or no season. I'm
expecting to spot a whopper today."

[138]

"Who'd bring it in?" Charley Joe asked. "Most of the men have gone over to Beaufort to sell yesterday's catch of mullet. You'd as well go on back home and sit by the fire. It's a cold day for May."

"Cold's nothing to me," Cap'n Willy replied. "These old arms may be past throwing a mean harpoon, but there's nothing wrong with my eyesight." He raised a shining spyglass and sighted far out beyond the breakers. "All clear and calm. Say, boy, ain't you supposed to be down on shore with the other lads, scraping hulls and polishing oars?"

"M-m," Charley Joe grunted. "Cap'n Willy, you don't really expect to spot a whale today, do you?"

"Never can tell, lad." The old man shouted his reply above the whine of the chilly spring wind, as he settled himself more comfortably. "No accounting for what those mighty critters may do. Let's see, the last one we took was —was—about—?"

"More'n a month gone," Charley Joe supplied the answer. "The 'Tom Rose Whale.' A big one all right. Seventy-five barrels of oil and seven hundred pounds of whalebone. Came to something like forty dollars a share, Pa said. It'll likely be the last one for this year, but we on Cape Lookout have had a right good season at that. Five whales in one year's a pretty fair catch, my grandsire says."

Thrusting his hands into his jacket pockets, kicking at shells as he went, Charley Joe ambled toward the shore where the fifteen other big boys from the village were busily preparing the whaleboats for storing until another year.

February, March, and April were whaling season off Cape Lookout, but March seemed to have ended the run this year, and the men had gone back to fishing, leaving the boys to ready the four big whaleboats for storage. The weather had been warm and balmy, but the sudden cold snap had made the air chilly. The boys were working fast to keep comfortable.

Charley Joe joined the others, who were busy with metal scrapers, raking the slime and scale from the hulls of the twenty-five-foot boats that were lined up on the sand. Big wooden tubs of rope, boat-spades, lances, and toggle-irons were piled neatly nearby.

"Old Cap'n Willy's up in the lookout, spotting as usual," Charley Joe remarked to Tod. "Says he expects a big one today. The old fellow must be getting a mite balmy."

"Who? Cap'n Willy?" Tod asked. "Not on your life. If Cap'n Willy thinks to see a whale blow today, it's more'n likely one will. He may be getting on in years, but Cap'n's sharp as a tack. I heard him tell my pa this morning that the men had better stay in port today, but Pa just laughed."

"S'pos'n a big one should spout. What would we do, with most of the men gone?"

"I reckon we boys would just have to man the boats and bring 'er in," Tod answered, scraping away at a stubborn patch of crust stuck tightly to the hull on which he was working. "Don't stand there chewing blubber, C. J. Get busy. We're s'posed to have at least two of these whaleboats clean by sunset. Not that it will do much good, if we're going to have to use them today."

"Aw, shucks!" Charley Joe was not at all eager to begin the hard, dirty work of scraping a hull. "Shucks! I'd as soon be manning oar as scraping hull. It's no harder work."

"Well, get at it anyway. Hey, Ab," Tod spoke to another boy. "What are you going to buy with your share of the whale?"

"What whale?" asked the husky redhead who was drawing his scraper with long, sure strokes down the side of a boat, walking along as he worked.

"The one we boys bring in today. C. J. says Cap'n Willy is looking for a whopper to blow this morning." Tod laughed mockingly.

"Aw, Tod. You crazy or something? You and C. J. know whale season's past, or else why would we be cleaning the boats? Pa said there wasn't a chance for another one this year." Ab was intent on his work.

"I think I'll buy me a sharpie with my share," Tod said to himself as much as to Charley Joe and Ab. "A trim little craft with two snow-white sails. Maybe I'll run you over to Beaufort in her, Ab. You, too, C. J."

Charley Joe snorted, and Ab said scornfully, "Yeah? I'll hold my breath till you do. Do you know, my pa's kept count and he's helped kill fifty-two whales since he was a grown man? I bet none of yours have got in on that many. Some of those whales took half a day to turn topside."

"You mean one of them did," Charley Joe said. "I've heard tell all about the 'Mayflower Whale.'"

"Well, my mama has helped boil down oil from more'n a million pounds of blubber," Tod bragged.

"My grandsire Hancock has cut out more baleen than anybody," Charley Joe boasted. "If it wasn't for him none of the ladies in the whole United States would have any whalebone for their collars and dress-stiffening. He keeps his baleen-axe keener than any razor."

Working and bragging, the boys were startled to hear the shout from Lookout Hill.

"Thar she blows!" It came loud and clear, and all the boys stopped at once and stood still, not believing their ears.

"Thar she blows!" They heard Cap'n Willy trumpet again through the megaphone of his cupped hands. "Thar she blows!"

The boys dropped their tools and started flinging the gear into the boats. The few men from the village came running and everybody worked like lightning.

Captain Sam, whale-gun in hand, directed the launching and soon the four boats were sliding over the sand toward the water.

"It's a good thing Captain Sam stayed at home today," Charley Joe puffed, as he pushed. "Or who would have shot the bomb-gun?"

"I could have," boasted Ab. "My pa's a captain, too, and he's showed me how, plenty of times."

"Yeah?" chorused several boys, laughing loudly. "You handle a harpoon-bomb-gun? Like fun!"

Ab paid no attention to the jeers but kept shoving with a strong shoulder against one of the moving boats. Some of the boys lifted the heavy tubs of harpoon rope into the boats as they moved toward the water, while others grabbed oars, ready to jump aboard and start for the whale. They could see the rising spume as the huge head surfaced some distance out.

"It's a big one!" shouted Captain Sam. "All together, lads! Pull for your life!" The first boat shot into the water.

In almost no time the four boats, rowed by the strong arms of the sixteen boys, were swooping through the waves toward the monstrous creature that had spouted beyond the breakers.

"Yipe-ee-ee!" shouted Ab, scarcely able to hang on to his oar for bouncing up and down with excitement. "Yipe-ee-ee, let me at 'er!"

The man in the second boat handled the other bomb-gun owned by the whalers of Diamond City, while the one man in each of the third and fourth boats carried the toggle-irons to use in case the guns failed to finish off the whale quickly enough.

Charley Joe found himself first oar in Captain Sam's boat with Tod opposite and Ab just behind him. Ab kept on whooping "Yipe-ee-ee! Yipe-ee-ee!" until the captain turned and silenced him with a stern look.

"Do you want the whale to hear you?" Charley Joe asked over his shoulder. "You know a crew has to keep quiet or it won't come up and spout nearby."

"Aw, what do you know about it?" Tod said, just as a gigantic black head, which looked bigger than any house in Diamond City, arose just in front of them, and a shower of spume soaked them all with salty foam.

Captain Sam raised the whale-gun and fired. The second boat drew alongside and its headman started to fire, but they had to pull away to keep from being hit by the great beast's sixteen-foot-wide tail. The monster sounded, its enormous tail threshing the air and churning the boats about as if they were leaves in a whirlwind. As it dived, the line, attached to the harpoon that was fast in its shoulder, uncoiled from the tub and played out so rapidly that it began to smoke as it rushed across the rail.

"Wet the line! Wet it down!" shouted the captain, and Tod let go his oar to dip up water with a pail, as fast as he could, to pour over the hissing rope.

"Another line!" commanded Captain Sam, when it looked as if the whale would take the whole fifty fathoms of rope from the first tub. But just then the line began to slacken, bubbles rose to the surface some distance ahead and a wavering mist of reddish spume shot into the air as the whale surfaced once more.

"Fire her!" bellowed Captain Sam, and the man with the other gun let go his harpoon-bomb. The shot found its mark, and the monster sounded again, only to come up more quickly than before. A wave of bloody salt water splattered on the men and boys in the boats, and a widening circle of red spread about the huge head now pushing to the surface for air.

"Close in!" roared the captain, although the other boats were already fighting the waves to get near enough for the hand-harpooners to thrust their irons into the giant beast of the sea.

"We've got 'er! We've got 'er! She's rolling!" Charley Joe dropped his oar and sprang up to shout the words, then felt himself flung violently into the slimy bilge in the bottom of the boat. At the same moment he glimpsed the mammoth tail of the dying whale towering over them like a huge black parasol and felt the boat rise up on one side. "We're goners!" he gasped and grabbed for his oar.

Miraculously, the boat righted itself and he saw the

other boats bobbing up and down, the men fighting with their oars to keep afloat.

The white underpart of the tremendous creature slowly turned upward on the surface of the waves, and soon the boatmen had strong lines attached to its tail. While some of the boys rowed steadily, the others grasped the lines and towed the huge body shoreward to beach it on the sand.

"Reckon we'll have to call this one the 'Little Children Whale,'" remarked Captain Sam, as his boat grated on the sandy beach and all jumped out to tug at the ropes attached to the monster. "Not that you boys are children," he hastened to add. "You lads behaved like grown men today, but we have to call it something. We lookouters name all our catches, you know."

"The 'Little Children Whale.' Why, that's a fine name for this mighty catch." Cap'n Willy had joined the group at the water's edge. "The 'Little Children Whale,'" he repeated. "That has a downright pleasing sound."

"Humph!" grunted Charley Joe. "It ought to have a better name than that."

Young teen-age boys were not usually allowed to go out in the whaleboats, as the capture of one of the monsters was a risky and dangerous undertaking. But, because most of the men were away that day, the boys of Diamond City did bring in a whale that has been known ever since as the "Little Children Whale."

Whaling was never the big business off the North Carolina coast that it was, and is, in the arctic and antarctic. It did, however, furnish the fishermen living in the shadow of the 160-foot-high Diamond Light on Cape Lookout with excitement and some extra income over a period of a century and a half. It was probably more the promise of excitement than the hope of profit that caused the fishermen of Diamond City to ready their gear and go after the whales every February when the big ones began their regular run past the Outer Banks.

For some unknown reason the whales stopped running that way in numbers, and the hurricanes along the eastern seaboard became more violent. In fact, one of the big winds practically blew Diamond City off the map in 1899, and whaling in North Carolina waters came to an end soon thereafter.

Although the whale's chase, capture, and processing on the shores of Cape Lookout ended with the end of the nineteenth century, its story is a fascinating chapter in the history of North Carolina. As a reminder of the days of whaling in the state, one can see, in the Museum of Natural History in Raleigh, the skeletons of three whales taken off the Outer Banks. Also on display is a complete set of gear used in such captures, along with the large iron pots and other equipment needed for processing the catch.

TOBACCO
AND BUCK DUKE

THE SOUND OF THE WIND THROUGH THE TALL PINE TREES HAD A
soothing effect on Buck Duke, eight years old. He lay
in the rickety old farm wagon, looking up to where the
bright blue sky almost rested at the edge of the tree tops.
Occasionally a few fluffy clouds came between the green
pine needles and the blue sky. Buck imagined that if his
arm were long enough, he could push his fingers right
through the clouds.

Up front, driving the two old blind mules, was his father,
Washington Duke. His father and he had got up very
early that morning, after a night spent camping near a
spring. They had been at the crossroads store at sunrise,
selling the little bags of tobacco they had brought from their
farm near Durham's Station.

All they had in the wagon was some cotton and those tiny

[147]

bags of tobacco. Of course, they had their camping equipment, too: some blankets, a few tin cups and plates, some bacon and corn meal, and feed for the mules. They were not paying for any hotels or restaurants! No, sir, this was a selling trip. Buck liked to sell things even more than his father did.

"Giddap!" shouted Buck's father to the blind mules.

Buck was almost asleep, lulled by the rocking motion of the wagon on the soft sandy road.

Buck's eyes blinked. "Where is our next stop?" he mumbled to his father.

"There's a little town down this road, where we're sure to get rid of what tobacco we have left. Then we can go back home. I want to stop by Raleigh and sell this cotton I swapped those sacks of flour for. Maybe we can buy some sugar to take to the other children."

Buck's mouth watered as he thought of sugar. The year was 1865. The war was just over, but not many people yet had enough money to pay the high price that sugar cost. The mention of sugar made Buck wide awake. He sat up, wiggled his bare feet in the straw of the wagon, put on his torn straw hat, and jumped over to sit by his father on the plank stretched from one side of the wagon to the other.

It was pleasant being there on the wagon with his father. When Washington Duke went away to be a soldier in the Confederate army, all of the children were sent over to Alamance County to live with their relatives. Buck's mother had died when he was two. He did not remember her at all. While he had liked living with his relatives—going to school a few months in the winter, helping with the tobacco crop in the summer, and attending the Methodist Church on Sundays—it was not the same as being at home. Then one day not long ago, his father had driven up with these two old blind mules and had taken his brother, his sister, and him back to the farm near Durham's Station.

Buck remembered the stories his father told him. Near the end of the war, Washington Duke had been made a prisoner by the northern soldiers. He was soon set free, made his way to New Bern, and then walked the entire 137 miles home. The only thing he had was a 50-cent piece, which he had exchanged with a Federal soldier for a worthless $5.00 Confederate bill. He found his 300-acre farm in ruins. The soldiers, both southern and northern, had stripped it of everything except a small storage shed of leaf tobacco, which they had overlooked.

Washington Duke, before going to war, had had a feeling that tobacco would be in demand after the fighting was over, so he had stored the tobacco to help him start a new life. The selling trip they were now on, down into the eastern part of North Carolina, would never have been possible if the soldiers had discovered and hauled away that stock of tobacco.

Near the end of the war—only a few months ago— soldiers from both armies had come into Durham's Station, seized J. R. Green's tobacco factory, and taken off as much of the crushed bright yellow weed as they could. It was so much better than any they had ever smoked that later, from their home states, they wrote back for more of the same product.

With the demand for tobacco so great, the children were hardly home with their father before he put the boys to work, while their twelve-year-old sister did the cooking and cleaning at the two-story frame house. People were saying that times were hard—but not Buck. Since there was no machinery, Washington Duke, with the help of his sons Ben and Buck, beat the tobacco with flails, then stuffed it into little bags. On each homemade bag they put a label, "Pro Bono Publico," Latin words meaning "For the public good." Smokers had to roll their own cigarettes from the tobacco in the bags.

Now, as Buck recalled these events, he saw ahead, beyond the pine trees, the outskirts of a small town. The blind mules soon were drawing the wagon along the dusty street to the center of the village. Buck and his father tied the mules to a hitching post, then announced their wares to the men who strolled along the sidewalk. Before two hours had passed, as Washington Duke had predicted, they had sold the last of their bags of tobacco. At this point, except for that final stop in Raleigh, they could go home.

Back on the farm, there was sugar for the children, and for Washington Duke, there was more money than he had dreamed he could make from the selling trip. Father and sons, he decided, would henceforth become tobacco merchants.

Near their house was a one-room log cabin, some twenty feet by thirty feet in size. In it they started their first tobacco factory. The boys were joined by their older half-brother Brodie, and the business grew rapidly. Buck resented even the time he had to spend at school in Durham's Station, but he knew an education was necessary if he was to be successful in life. What he really enjoyed were the selling trips with his father, though now they traveled in a large canvas-covered wagon drawn by strong horses. Later he made himself leave home for more education at Guilford College and at a business school in New York state.

When James Buchanan Duke (though everybody called him Buck) was fourteen, his father made him manager of the little tobacco factory on the farm. Three years later, their output was so great that they moved from the farm and set up a large plant in Durham's Station where they were near the railroad.

A year later, when Buck was eighteen, Washington Duke made the boys his partners, and thus was born the firm of W. Duke & Sons. Buck was the businessman of the firm; he knew *everything* about tobacco, for he had started at the bottom. He knew about growing tobacco, buying it, packaging it, and selling it. As a boy, he had learned how to work fourteen hours a day, cut expenses, and save money for expansion.

Before he was thirty, he was a millionaire. And when, in 1890, the firm of W. Duke & Sons became the American Tobacco Company, James B. Duke was head of one of the largest tobacco operations in the world.

It is said that he had money to burn, but he neither burned it nor wasted it. He put his tobacco earnings into building dams and power companies in North and South Carolina. By the time of his death in 1925, he had provided enough money to change Trinity College, a struggling Methodist institution, into our present Duke University. There was money left over to lend support to hospitals, country churches, and other colleges.

Today, one may visit the Duke homestead and the tiny tobacco factory on the old Duke farm near Durham. Not far away, at the center of the Duke University campus, a statue of James B. Duke stands just in front of the towering Duke Chapel.

A BEAUTY AND A BEAST
IN THE
WORLD OF WILDFLOWERS

NORTH CAROLINA IS SAID TO HAVE A GREATER VARIETY OF PLANT
life than any other state in the Union. From the showy
purple and white rhododendron in the mountains to the rare
pitcher-plants in the east, from the old towering balsams
on Clingman's Dome to the rustling palmetto on the Outer
Banks, this state is a botanist's paradise.
It boasts more varieties of trees than all
of Europe and has within its boundaries
more than 1,300 species of wildflowers.

Two of the rarest plants in the world
are natives of North Carolina. The dainty,
white, bell-flowered shortia, with its small,
scalloped, thick green leaves resembling
galax, grows only in the high mountains
of the beautiful Sapphire Country, spill-
ing over into a small area of South Caro-

[153]

lina and Georgia. It is found nowhere else in the world
except Japan. The other curiosity of the plant world is the
insect-eating Venus'-flytrap, whose only native habitat is
the boggy soil of Brunswick and adjoining counties and a
tiny area across the line in South Carolina.

The story of the discovery of beautiful *Shortia galacifolia,* sometimes called Oconee-bells or one-flower colts-
foot, and of its hundred years of obscurity is a romantic
tale in itself.

In 1794 the famous French botanist, André Michaux,
who had been gathering specimens in eastern North America for some years, sailed for home with an enormous collection of trees, shrubs, and dried and mounted wildflowers
and plants. The sailing ship *Ophir* on which he traveled
had a stormy crossing and was wrecked in a gale off the
coast of Holland. When Michaux realized that the ship
was doomed, he lashed himself and as many of his precious
bundles as he could to a plank to await the end. As the
ship heaved and groaned, fast on the rocks and pounded by
wind and waves, the little *Ophir* began to break up, and
Michaux was tossed into the sea.

When he came to, he found himself on shore, and,
miraculously, his valuable bundles were scattered about
him. While he recovered from his near-drowning, kind
people helped him wash and clean his water-soaked specimens and remount them on fresh paper. He finally reached
France and gave his collection to the Jardin des Plantes in
Paris. Here it lay neglected for almost half a century after
André Michaux's death.

In 1839 a young American botanist named Asa Gray was
visiting all of the famous botanical collections in Europe in

preparation for writing his large work on the flora of North America. At the Jardin des Plantes he sought out the neglected American collection of the celebrated André Michaux. Examining the mounted specimens of wildflowers, Dr. Gray spied a small dried-up bunch of leaves with a seed pod attached that for some unknown reason greatly fired his imagination. In all his wanderings in his homeland he had not seen anything like it. But the specimen bore no name, only a note saying it had been found in the high mountains of North Carolina. Dr. Gray determined that he would find out more about the new plant and its habitat and locate it when· he returned to America.

Thus began a search that lasted more than forty years. After looking for a long while in France, he located Michaux's diary—what was left of it—and, to his great delight, read in the crumpled, water-stained pages a description of the little plant. He found that Michaux had gathered, on the slopes of a high mountain in North Carolina and at the meeting of two rivers where a trail led into the forest, "a small, woody, creeping plant with saw-toothed leaves resembling the galax, though more dainty." It covered the moist, acid soil beneath the shade of the mountain laurels, and the Indians whose village lay nearby said it had a good taste when chewed and a pleasing odor when crushed. Nowhere else had he ever seen its like, wrote the French botanist.

Now Dr. Gray was more excited than ever about the plant, and since it was unnamed, he decided to give it a name. As it must grow near Kentucky, he thought, he would call it *Shortia* in honor of the pioneer Kentucky botanist, Dr. Charles Wilkins Short. Since its leaves re-

sembled the galax he added the designation, *galacifolia.*
Little did Dr. Gray dream that he would spend the rest of
his life trying to get one look at the unknown flower of the
new plant. He made many trips to North Carolina from
Boston, where he was teaching and working at Harvard
University, but there are many high mountains in the state
and he always missed the one high mountain he sought.
On none of the slopes did he find a single plant of shortia,
nor could he find anyone in all Appalachia who could lead
him to one. He did find, however, in an ancient Japanese
plant book, a plant that resembled his shortia, and he at
least had a picture of its flowers.

Dr. Gray continued his search year after year and was
joined by other enthusiastic botanists, but it seemed use-
less until one day a specimen of the long-sought shortia
came to him in the mail. It had been found by a young
boy, George Hyams, on the banks of the Catawba River near
Marion, North Carolina. Young Hyams' father was a
herbalist, but he had never seen the plant before. He sent
it to a friend to identify, and the friend sent it on to Dr. Gray
for classifying. After almost forty years, Dr. Asa Gray held
in his hands a living specimen of the plant for which he
had searched so long. But there were no flowers accom-
panying the small, round, thick, saw-toothed leaves. Dr.
Gray and his wife made the long trip from Boston to
North Carolina once more to see the plant actually growing,
but the time was autumn, not blossoming season, and the
place was not a high mountain as Michaux had written.
Asa Gray continued to seek the flower.

Finally, as he grew older and unable to travel so far, Dr.
Gray turned the search over to Dr. Charles Sprague Sargent,

professor of arborculture at Harvard University, who was as eager as Dr. Gray to find the original spot mentioned by Michaux. Dr. Sargent camped in the Lake Toxaway region, and one day, in the pouring rain, at the meeting of the Toxaway and Horsepasture Rivers, he came upon a faint trail. He remembered that Michaux's journal had mentioned an Indian trail, so he followed the long-unused path. It led down instead of up. Could the botanist of nearly a century ago have meant "among the mountains," instead of "on the mountains?" Michaux had meant just that, for at a height of only 1,500 feet, Sargent came upon a bed of the little woody plants beneath the mountain laurels, just as the French botanist had described them. Again, it was not the blossoming season but autumn, and so there were no flowers. Sargent dug up a specimen from the very spot where André Michaux had discovered shortia ninety-eight years before, and sent it to Dr. Gray. His joy was great, but still his fondest wish was unfulfilled. He could not be completely happy until he could fully describe both the lost plant and its flowers.

In May one of the Sargent party returned to the Sapphire Country to secure some blossoming specimens, but he could not remember just where the plants were located. Fortunately, he found the guide who had been with them the autumn before. In a short while they came upon "masses of dainty, little, white, fringed bells, each swaying on its pink-tinged stem, rising about six inches from a rosette of glossy, green, scalloped leaves." The man quickly dug up a box of the blossoming plants, packed them carefully, and took them back to Dr. Gray. It is said the seventy-eight-year-old botanist cried with joy when he beheld the little flowers he had sought for so many years. Now he could fully describe the little lost plant, whose only habitat in North America is The Land of the Sky.

In less than a year after realizing his fifty-year dream, Dr. Asa Gray died on January 30, 1888, and his colleagues covered his grave with a living blanket of *Shortia galacifolia,* the one plant he loved best of the more than 25,000 he had studied and classified.

No one knows why *Shortia galacifolia* grows in only a few spots nor why it never seems to spread. It can be transplanted, and a few nurseries specializing in wildflowers offer it for sale, but it usually dies in a domestic situation. Dr. B. W. Wells of North Carolina State University at Raleigh suggests that shortia is a "lingering survival of another botanical age, and is on its way to extinction." Whatever it may be, *Shortia galacifolia,* the plant that was lost a hundred years, is one of the most beautiful of all wildflowers and one of the rarest.

In direct contrast to the dainty mountain-dweller, shortia, there grows in the low, marshy soil of southeastern North Carolina one of the most astonishing members of the wild flower world. It is the unbelievable Venus'-flytrap, which devours ants, gnats, flies, caterpillars, worms, small grasshoppers, and even tiny frogs. It's a perfect beast of a plant.

The Venus'-flytrap likes the moist, semi-boggy ground on the edge of the sandhills near Wilmington and a small area of similar soil at the edge of South Carolina. It has been found native in no other place in the whole world. It grows from four to twelve inches high, coming up in early April, puts out white blossom-topped spikes in May, and matures in about three months. It reseeds itself and dies down in autumn, only to start its life cycle over again the next spring.

This strange insect-eating plant, which seems almost like a creature from another world, has long, green leaves in a rosette close to the ground. Each leaf bears at its tip a pair of bright red lobes that work like the two jaws of a clam shell. These bristle-fringed jaws remain invitingly open, spread bright and red in the sun, until some careless insect touches the sensitive hairs and triggers the mechanism that makes them snap shut and ensnare the poor victim. The jaws press gently at first, then squeeze harder and harder until the helpless captive dies from pressure. The digestive juices secreted in the miniature stomach go to work, and in five to ten days, the skeleton is expelled and the trap opens wide to await another meal.

Strange as it may seem, wood, metal, and paper will not trigger the jaws of the plant. Those deadly lobes will take in only the live creatures upon which the Venus'-flytrap feeds. Rosily inviting in the sunlight, they seem to have a fatal fascination for small live things. Unlike the sundew, the pitcher-plant, and the trumpet-flower, which only snare their victims with a sticky substance, the Venus'-flytrap grabs hers and eats them.

Because of its narrow range, its shallow root system, and its spectacular behavior, the Venus'-flytrap was threatened with extinction some years ago. Drainage of its swampy home was a threat, but man was a greater danger. Commercial outfits began digging up the rare plants and peddled them about the country as curiosities, which they certainly are. This was stopped by a law passed in 1951 that prevents taking the plant from its natural habitat. The rarity is saved for the time being.

Perhaps the Venus'-flytrap, like shortia, is also a survival from another botanical age, and it also is on its way to extinction.

BREAD,
BEAUTY, AND BROTHERHOOD

"NO MATTER HOW GREAT THE SEEMING OBSTACLES NOW, I SHALL become a writer and shall make it my life's work."

A young Chatham County farm boy of fourteen set that goal for himself one day in 1896. Clarence Poe did become a writer. He also became a crusader. At the age of eighty, Dr. Poe said the greatest tribute ever paid to him was that of a farmer who declared, "You have put more bread and meat in folks' mouths than anybody else in the South."

Although Clarence Poe did not go to college, he was an educated man. During his lifetime he received more honors than even he could have dreamed of when, as a North

Carolina lad, he staked out his claim to the future. Five colleges and universities gave him doctorates, the highest honor they can bestow. Being included in the Hall of Fame of Great Americans is reserved only for the most outstanding men, and Clarence Poe was given a place among them in 1925. Other great organizations praised and rewarded him. The American Freedom Association presented him the World Peace Award in 1926, and his own state gave him one of its first North Carolina Awards for public service. There were so many other honors that we cannot mention them all.

He was a friend of presidents, from Teddy Roosevelt through Dwight Eisenhower; and even kings entertained him when he traveled. Never has a boy fulfilled his own plans more completely than this scholar and gentleman who from the age of sixteen spent his life writing and speaking for the betterment of his fellow men, especially southern farmers.

As editor of *The Progressive Farmer,* a post he held for sixty-four years, Dr. Poe's writings touched millions of farm people. He wrote in behalf of better farming, good roads, and education and health for rural people. He urged higher standards of living, beautification of the land, and peace and brotherhood for all. When he became its editor on July 4, 1899, at the age of eighteen, *The Progressive Farmer* was a small weekly paper with a circulation of 5,000. When he died on October 8, 1964, at the age of eighty-three, still senior editor, *The Progressive Farmer* was a beautiful, thick, monthly magazine. It was printed in five separate editions in as many states, with over 1,500,000 subscribers. From the time Dr. Poe bought the magazine in 1903 until the end of his life, he never once wavered from his declared purpose to make of it a guide for better country life.

To understand this outstanding North Carolinian and his wide influence on the state's agriculture, let us look back at farmers and farming before the time of Clarence Poe and *The Progressive Farmer.*

In colonial days, land was the principal form of wealth in North Carolina, and farming was the main occupation of the people. Most of the settlements were along the eastern half of the Coastal Plain and in the Piedmont, with sparsely populated pine forests and sand barrens between. Only a few bold homesteaders dared brave the dangers of the Cherokee Indians and the rough land of the mountainous western section. The majority of settlers in the east and Piedmont were small farmers with few or no slaves.

After the Revolution, by 1783, when slavery had become very important in our state, some smart landlords had become the owners of large plantations of 10,000 or more acres each. Almost all of these large plantations were along the boundaries of the Cape Fear, Tar, and Roanoke Rivers. These men who owned the land were known as "the gentry," and they had many slaves to labor for them. They and their families lived lives of comfort, ease, and social grace.

A far larger portion of the population was made up of small farmers who engaged in what is known as subsistence farming. This means that they were barely able to keep alive on what they earned. They owned few or no slaves. Members of a third class, called artisans, were small merchants, blacksmiths, gunsmiths, overseers, livestock dealers, and tavern-keepers. From the lower classes of artisans, there sprung a fourth group, called by the Negroes "po' white trash." The descendants of this class, along with many freed slaves, became tenant farmers.

Colonial farmers learned most of their farming practices from the Indians, who did little about conserving the land and its resources. If a field of maize yielded a poor crop one year, the Indian cleared a new field for the next season and abandoned the old. Colonial farmers did the same, and so did their immediate descendants. Such a system led to a great waste of soil and forests. Farmers made very little effort to restore fertility to worn-out fields by enriching the soil and rotating crops. They cut over large forest areas, ruthlessly clearing them for "new ground," and burned them to ensure fresh grass for their livestock that roamed at large. "The colonial farmer was a great waster of natural resources," stated one historian.

By 1835 conditions in North Carolina agriculture had changed but little. Farming was still the principal source of livelihood for the majority. Though some attempts had been made to upgrade farm practices and improve livestock, the farmer held on to his old, back-breaking, wasteful methods of cultivating the land. The plantation owner had no especial reason to change, as he had plenty of slaves to labor for him. The small independent farmer did not choose to change. He was satisfied with little or no education, poor roads, and old-time methods of cultivating by hand. Many were superstitious and followed such practices as "planting by the moon."

Before 1860 public schools were few and widely separated. They ran for a few months each year and were attended only by boys and girls whose parents were especially eager for them to learn. Not many children had such parents, for in 1854 there were 73,566 white North Carolinians over the age of twenty who could not read or write. Travel was difficult for there was not a single road in the state that could be used in all kinds of weather. Since farmers could not get surpluses to market, many of them saw no reason to grow more produce than they needed for themselves. Most farmers had no use for agricultural societies or farm journals that advocated "book-farming." Only the more ambitious farmers in rural areas dared to try new ways. Still there was some progress, for a copy of the *Farmers' Journal* of 1854 declared that "North Carolina is shaking off her dullness and entering upon an era of improvement and progress in farm practices."

Then came the Civil War.

At the end of four years of fighting, the South was exhausted, especially North Carolina. She had lost more young men than any other southern state and had suffered battles, Sherman's march, and the poverty that war brings.

Many plantations had been plundered and slave labor, rightly, was no more. The small farmer's work animals had been driven off. His smokehouse was swept bare, and even the salt that had dripped on the floorboards was gone. His fields were destroyed. It was easy for him to sink back into the old indifference and take up where his grandfather and great-grandfather had left off, forgetting any progress his father might have made. He plowed his barren field with himself hitched to the broken plow, while his wife held the reins. His children did not go to school. He planted "by the moon," if weather permitted, or did not plant at all. It was easy for such a farmer to give in to defeat and argue that what was good enough for his ancestors was good enough for him and his family. While some farmers recovered their ambitions rather quickly and began the rugged climb to prosperity, many more did not.

Where there had been 75,203 farms in North Carolina in 1860, there were three times that many in 1900, with almost half of these worked by tenant farmers, white and Negro. Thousands of slaves had been liberated in the state, most of whom knew no other way of making a living than by working in fields as tenants or hired hands. Hired hands sometimes got as much as fifty cents a day, and tenant farmers nearly always found themselves deep in debt at the end of the year. Toward this group who were bewildered and struggling, young Clarence Poe began in 1900 to direct his crusade for rural betterment.

Born into a situation of culture, some prosperity, and peace, he saw around him men living in poverty who had been slaves and those who had owned slaves. In the course of his growing up he watched their struggles and hardships and was inspired to fight for their betterment. He determined that he would do his best to put fertility into their barren soil, good livestock in their barns, and better crops in their fields. He resolved to work for better roads, better schools, and better churches in rural communities, better health and more beauty in farm homes, and a measure of prosperity in the lives of all country people. To this end, young Poe set out to prepare himself. He read everything he could find about farming, especially *The Progressive Farmer*.

At the time that Clarence Poe wrote out for himself his declaration of his intended life's work (quoted at the beginning of this story), he began writing articles for the county newspapers and for *The Progressive Farmer*. This small journal had been founded in Winston-Salem in 1886 by Colonel L. L. Polk and later was moved to Raleigh. When he was sixteen, Poe wrote a moving article about more taxes for public schools, in which he said that The Old North State was near the bottom of the ladder in the matter of public education. He sent it to *The Progressive Farmer* and enclosed a note saying that he hoped to be an editor himself one day. J. L. Ramsey, who was then editor, was impressed with the article and with the fact that it was written by a sixteen-year-old boy. He sent for Poe and offered him a job as his assistant. Clarence accepted eagerly. Now he was in a position to present his ideas of better farming and farm life by educating children, balancing production, and raising up-graded livestock.

He started his lifelong crusade for what he called "Two-armed farming, and culture with agriculture." At that time, around 1900, cotton was king in the entire South. One of Poe's first articles as an assistant editor declared that the southern farmer could make progress only by planting a variety of crops and by raising better and even better livestock.

Two years later, only eighteen, Poe chose to accept the editorship of *The Progressive Farmer* instead of going to college. He felt that to carry on his crusade for rural betterment through its pages, and to stick to his motto of "Fight for the underdog," was more important than to obtain further education for himself. He also felt that having the State Library right there in Raleigh, where he could read every minute of his spare time, was almost as good as going to college. He made full use of the library.

In later years when influential men urged Clarence Poe to become a candidate for Governor of North Carolina, with almost certain election, he refused because he felt it more important to stay with *The Progressive Farmer*.

It would take a separate story to list all of the crusades for betterment of rural dwellers, and for world peace and brotherhood, that Clarence Poe engaged in by writing and speaking during the sixty-five years he edited his journal. A few examples will give an idea of his widespread influence on agriculture in North Carolina.

First, last, and always, he begged for conservation of the soil by rotation of crops, fertilization, prevention of erosion, and balancing of crops with livestock. He wrote, spoke, and traveled on behalf of securing better health, better roads, and better schools with compulsory attendance laws and equality of education for *every* child. He campaigned for beauty in homes, in churches, and along highways. He promoted home and farm demonstration work and clubs for boys and girls in rural communities. From his Tomato Clubs for girls and Tobacco Clubs for boys there grew the widespread, honored, and important Four-H Clubs of the present day. Dr. Poe's interests in behalf of farmers and farm families, whatever their race, creed, or color, were unbounded. He spent his long and fruitful life to project and spread his ideas.

In the 1960's, as in colonial days, farming is still a major factor in North Carolina's economy, but with what a difference! On its 190,000 farms live the largest number of farm people of any state in the Union. On its 19,426,129 acres of farm land grow food, fiber, and wood to supply uncounted millions. In its farm homes electricity has taken the place of candles, kerosene, and back-breaking labor for women. In the fields and barns, automation has taken the place of oxen and mule-power. The state has one of the finest systems of highways and secondary roads in the land. These roads make it easy for the farmer to transport his produce to markets and supplies to his home, and they free him and his family from isolation. North Carolina is the fourth state in the nation in cash income from farm crops, first in tobacco production, second in peanut production, eighth in egg production, and first in home consumption of both crops and livestock.

The Old North State has come far in rural economy in the last hundred years. A large part of this progress is the result of one man's efforts. He dreamed of a better life for rural people in his state and elsewhere, and he spent his own life in sharing that dream.

Dr. Clarence Poe liked to quote his old friend, the poet Edwin Markham: "Man's supreme needs are three B's—Bread, Beauty, and Brotherhood," and Dr. Poe did his best to help the southern farmer satisfy those needs.

THE WRIGHT BROTHERS
AT KITTY HAWK

ON A DAY IN LATE SEPTEMBER, 1903, TWO BROTHERS GOT OFF THE train at Elizabeth City. In the baggage car was a peculiar contraption that they had made at their home in Dayton, Ohio. When assembled, it looked like a big kite. Although nobody paid much attention to the brothers and their contraption, the two Ohio men knew exactly what they planned to do with it. Wilbur Wright was thirty-six years old, Orville thirty-two. Both were blue-eyed and slender.

Loading their suitcases and their contraption onto a small boat, they began the slow trip across the waters of Albemarle Sound to the village of Kitty Hawk on the Outer Banks. The journey was not new to them, for this was their fourth trip to Kitty Hawk.

The year 1903 was to be the climax of much dreaming and planning. As boys back in Dayton, they had always been interested in inventing things. Their father, a bishop, encouraged them. Perhaps their wish to be inventors began when they received their first bicycles. Nothing would do but to see how the bicycles worked. Soon they knew so much about bicycles that they set up a small shop for repairing broken-down "bikes."

They might well have spent their lives as bicycle repair-men, if they had not read an article about some experiments in Germany with a glider. Now, as everyone knows, a glider is a sort of airplane without a motor. In the air, it moves only as the wind permits, as it has no power of its own. When the Wright brothers read about the glider, they began to imagine a new invention: a man-carrying glider with a bicycle motor to keep it going—even straight into the wind. This had never happened before.

On that September day in 1903, as they looked across the waters of Albemarle Sound, they wondered if this time, after so many failures, they would be able to rise into the air against the wind.

Man had long wanted to fly like a bird. Four hundred years before, the great Italian artist and scientist Leonardo da Vinci had sketched a design for a machine which might fly, but nothing had come of it. More recently other in-ventors had made other attempts. The Wright brothers knew about all of these efforts. They had read everything they could put their hands on, they had experimented with kites of all kinds, and they had sat for hours watching the flight of birds in the sky.

Finally had come the day when they were ready for their own experiment. They needed a flat, treeless coun-try with a few sandhills, they wanted strong, steady winds, and they demanded privacy. The weather bureau at Washington suggested that Kitty Hawk was such a place.

On their first visit in 1900, the Kitty Hawk villagers looked upon them as just a couple of "cranks" who wanted to fly a big kite. The brothers explained their business as little as necessary. At that time nobody thought flight was possible, and to try it would have been considered insane.

Yet in 1900 and the two years following, the two continued to test the effects of air currents on the wings of their gliders. From time to time, they improved their design. The men at the nearby Coast Guard station—and especially Captain "Bill" Tate—were helpful but not really too curious about what was going on. Since the brothers were always well-dressed, the Kitty Hawk men and women thought of them as pleasant, rich playboys fooling around with some big kites.

In 1902, after more than a thousand gliding flights at Kitty Hawk, the brothers went back to Dayton and made plans, at last, for a motor-driven plane that would carry a man.

As they neared the dock at Kitty Hawk the following September, they had with them the new contraption they had built during the winter and also a motor that they had designed and constructed in their bicycle shop. The plane, including the motor filled with fuel, weighed 745 pounds.

With the help of some of the fishermen who were at the dock at Kitty Hawk, the brothers took the plane and all their equipment across the sands to the unpainted shacks they had built the year before. One shack was a crude hangar for the plane, and the other served as living quarters. All of the expenses for their glider experiments had come from their own pockets. No one had wanted to invest money in some crazy notion about making a machine for a man to fly in.

As the autumn days followed one another, the Wright brothers repaired their shacks, assembled the parts of their plane, and waited for just the proper weather for flying. They built a sixty-foot lumber track on the sand to provide a smooth launching.

Over and over again, they tested the motor and tightened the joints of the queer contraption. Indeed, it was a strange looking object. Its two parallel kite-like wings had a span of more than forty feet, and the length of the plane from front to back was about twenty feet. The eight-horsepower motor of four cylinders was operated by bicycle chains. It was, as a matter of fact, merely a glider with a motor attached.

During the fall, the weather never seemed right, and months passed. Then, on December 14, the Wright brothers made a first attempt to get their plane into the air. When their effort was a failure, they spent two days making minor repairs to the plane.

The morning of December 17, 1903 (an important date!), the air was clear and cold and breezy. The wind was the kind they had been waiting for, a gale of twenty-five miles an hour, and it was from the north. They would try again. They signaled to the Coast Guard Station to send somebody over to their camp, and shortly there were a number of people grouped around the plane. One was a boy from Kitty Hawk village.

Since the brothers swapped about at the controls, and since it was Wilbur who had been on the plane three days before, it was Orville's turn. With the help of the men, the plane was put onto the wooden track, facing north into the wind. They waited until the air was just exactly right. The engine was wide open. A photographer stood in place. It was 10:30 in the morning.

The plane started sliding along the track with all of the men except the photographer pushing it to increase its speed. In the plane, Orville lay flat on his stomach as the plane moved forward and the engine roared. The men drew back, but Wilbur ran alongside, steadying a wing. Two-thirds of the way down the track, the plane suddenly rose 8 feet into the air, then 10 feet, and then it settled upon the ground 120 feet away. This plane had flown into the wind, not coasted along with it like every glider of the past.

Later Orville Wright wrote: "This flight lasted only 12 seconds, but it was nevertheless the first in the history of the world in which a machine carrying a man had raised itself by its own power into the air in full flight, had sailed forward without reduction of speed, and had finally landed at a point as high as that from which it started."

This flight had taken place at Kitty Hawk on the Outer Banks of North Carolina. A dream had come true. Immediately after this first flight, Wilbur took the controls and flew about 200 yards. A third attempt, with Orville in the plane, went the same distance. A fourth and last flight on that famous December day was Wilbur's. It lasted 59 seconds, went 852 feet, at 31 miles an hour. At the end of the flight, the plane ran into a sand dune. The wind turned the light contraption over and over and smashed the front rudder frame. There would be no more flights that December. The brothers then sent a message to their sister back in Dayton, Ohio: "Flight successful. Be home for Christmas."

In the years that followed, the Wright brothers designed and built many different airplanes, improving their models each time. But no flight was ever so important as the one that lasted 12 seconds, went 10 feet into the air, and flew only 120 feet away.

The site of the first flight near Kitty Hawk can be visited today. A beautiful granite monument stands atop a sandhill, now covered with grass. The actual spot where the first flight took place is nearby, and the two unpainted shacks have been rebuilt on the very ground where they once stood. Not far away is a museum containing a replica of the first Wright airplane.

CAPTAIN CAT

JANUARY 30, 1921, HAD BEEN A CLEAR DAY BUT VERY COLD, WITH a relatively calm sea, and all the men off duty at Cape Hatteras Coast Guard Station had stayed within the cozy circle of warmth around the pot-bellied stove in the main room. No distress signals nor cries for help had come from the shoals off Diamond.

"All calm! All clear! No trace of sail or smoke!" reported the last daylight watch, as he joined the others, hoping to settle down for a long night's sleep.

The nearby lighthouse blinked its regular warning flash across the treacherous Diamond Shoals, but no signal flares from any passing vessel flashed back from the Graveyard of the Atlantic. All seemed still and at peace for once on that stretch of ocean that had seen so many wrecks within the time of shipping along its lanes.

But a different cry came from the early daylight watch as he roused the crew at the first hazy streaks of chilling dawn on the morning of January 31. "Schooner aground on the outer shoal! Five-master! All sails set! Tugging at sand!"

The captain of the station rolled from his warm bunk, shouting orders as he threw on his clothes and his oilskins, "Man the boat! Roll her out! All hands on board!" The crew had the boat rolled over the sand and into the chopping waves in a matter of minutes.

"Look at her!" exclaimed the watch who had first seen the stranded vessel. "A five-master, and all sails set. Where's she from?"

"No sign of her last night," replied the evening watch.

"She's a ghostly sight," called another of the crew above the whine of the rising wind. "Like a spirit out of no-where."

"All sails set and full to the breeze!" shouted another, trying to outroar the waves. "Jib and topsail furled. Not trying to get off."

"New cloth, those sails," cried still another crewman. "And prow fast on Outer Diamond. Must be stuck in ten feet of sand."

The power lifeboat chugged toward the ghost-like but beautiful, new-looking five-masted schooner, just sitting there in eight feet of water as if she had been carefully placed by a giant hand. But the sea was growing rough, the waves running higher every moment, and the lifeboat could get no closer than a quarter of a mile.

The captain pulled out his glass and held it to an eye. "The *Carroll A. Deering,*" he reported to the crew. "Shipshape as the day she sailed, whenever that may have been. Not a soul in sight. Decks as clear as if they'd been swept." He handed the glass to another, and began to hallo through his megaphone.

"Ladder hanging over portside," said the crewman with the telescope. The captain called again and again but no figure appeared on the deck of the schooner to answer his shouts.

"The crew numbered ten or more at the least," said the captain. "But where are they all? It's plain they haven't tried to float her off the shoal with the jib and topsail not even unfurled."

"No boats on the davits," reported the crewman with the telescope. "Must've abandoned ship."

"Where'd they go, then?" said the captain. "It wasn't rough enough last night to swamp a sturdy lifeboat." He raised his megaphone and shouted again, but the only reply that came from the *Carroll A. Deering* was the rattle of the rigging in the chilling wind and the boiling of the waves lashing about her in the shallow shoals.

The Hatteras boat circled about the craft for several hours, but still could detect no sign of life aboard, nor could its crew see anything amiss on the stranded schooner.

"We'll make for shore, since we can't get to her," decided the captain, "and get more help."

Back at the Coast Guard Station, checking the *Marine Register,* they found that the *Carroll A. Deering* was a $200,000, five-masted schooner of 1,879 tons, built two years before at Bath, Maine, and that she regularly made cargo runs. The owner was notified of her predicament, and a cutter was requested from Wilmington to aid the three other nearby coast guard crews that were speeding to the rescue.

The weather grew rougher, seas ran higher, and breakers continued to roar over Diamond Shoals, keeping the rescuers away from the ghostly schooner for four full days after she was discovered. She remained there, her white sails still spread, sitting high out of the water like some great resting bird. Finally the deadly billows subsided enough for the coast guardsmen to approach and board the schooner.

"Well! Who? What? How?" exclaimed the bewildered captain when they had scuttled up the ladder still hanging over the rail. "Steering gear smashed! Looks like it was done on purpose."

"Aye, sir, with this sledge hammer here." A crewman gestured toward a heavy sledge hammer propped against the wheel. "The rudder's swinging, too. Not an anchor chain in sight."

The crewmen spread about the vessel and shouted their findings to the captain. "Signal flares unused! Stores all in order! Flags all shipshape!"

"Bunks made up," called another. "None of them slept in!"

"The instruments are missing," stated the man who was examining the skipper's berth. "Clock, barometer, captain's belongings all gone. Light's still burning in the saloon. Red and green running lights properly set."

After a thorough examination of everything topside, the captain of the coast guard led the way below and began a search inside the schooner. They finally entered the galley.

"By the great horn spoon!" exclaimed the captain. "The table set for mess! They left in a hurry, that's for sure!"

"Plenty of food cooked, too," said a man lifting a pot lid on top of the long-cold range. "Enough stew here to feed an army. Queer-smelling stuff." He opened and slammed shut the oven door. "Funny-looking bread in there. Not proper biscuit-stuff."

The captain opened the oven to take a look, and just then every man of them stopped dead still, frozen by the first sound they had heard aboard the *Carroll A. Deering* except the creaking of timbers and the flapping of sails.

"Avast!" whispered the captain. "Somebody!" He held up a hand to silence the crewmen beginning to breathe heavily and mumble. "Somebody moaning in pain."

The peculiar, drawn-out moan came again, at first seeming fairly close, somewhere outside the galley, then getting farther away, until it ceased entirely.

"Sounded like a body in deep pain," said one.

"Somebody sore hurt," added another. "But how could he move about if he was that bad off. I'd've sworn that first groan came from amongst the ballast. Listen! There it is again! Topside."

All hands rushed back up on deck and searched for the creature—man, animal, whatever it was—that had been crying so woefully, but not a sound could they hear from it now. The clash of the waves and the whistle of the wind had taken over once more.

A guardsman removed his sou'wester and ran his hand through his hair. "Ghost," he muttered, shaking his head. "Nothing but a ghost would play tag like that. Nothing but a ghost could have set this five-master down like this in the sand. Everything so shipshape and no human aboard."

Just then the tug *Rescue* from Norfolk came alongside, and her crew also combed the *Carroll A. Deering* from stem to stern, with no more results than the Hatterasmen.

While the skipper of the *Rescue* and the captain of Hatteras Station were discussing the whole weird situation in the cabin of the schooner's master, both their crews were going over the vessel for the third time.

"No wonder there were no distress flares seen last night," said the captain. "There just wasn't anyone aboard to send them aloft, when she fetched up on the shoals."

"Aye, and no helmsman to keep her from plowing onto them. It's mighty strange, though, mighty strange. We haven't had a real storm for some time. She couldn't have blown off course."

"Unless she lost her anchors in that squall off Cape Fear some days back. But that was too long ago—she—" The captain stopped in midsentence. "Hist! There's that moan again!" He sprang up from the chair beneath the light that cast weird shadows about the cabin with every movement of the ship. "Sounds as if it's right in this cabin, now. We heard it first when we were searching below, near the galley. Then it got away from us."

"Somebody in pain," replied the master of the *Rescue*.

"Or a ghost," mumbled the captain under his breath, peering about.

"It *is* in this cabin." The *Rescue's* skipper pointed, "There!"

"Whatever it is, I'll have it out of here!" The captain lifted the dun-colored blanket hanging over the side of the bunk and pulled from underneath it a lean dark cat, with blazing green eyes. It was gaunt and trembling but spitting and hissing, and it was not too weak to give its rescuer a nasty scratch across his hand.

The captain held the terrified animal at arm's length for a moment, exclaiming in disgust, "Ghost!" Then he drew it toward him and tried to soothe the frightened creature.

Suddenly the skipper of the *Rescue* burst into a roar of laughter. "Captain Cat!" he shouted with glee, slapping his hands on his slicker-clad knees. "So that's the captain of the *Carroll A. Deering*! Captain Cat!"

As it was impossible for the *Carroll A. Deering* to be floated off the shoal, all of her usable gear, rigging, sails, ropes, furniture, and everything of value was salvaged and sold at auction, while the winds and the waves began their work of breaking her to pieces. On March 21, a portion of the wreckage floated down toward Ocracoke and settled there in the shifting sands. The gulls, who had chosen the remnant for a roosting and a nesting place, squawked and cried about the piece of hull. Superstitious folks began declaring that they could see spirits walking about the poop deck and striding atop the battered pilot-house. The *Carroll A. Deering* was declared a ghost ship.

Many investigations were made to try to discover the fate of the crew of the *Carroll A. Deering,* but nothing significant was ever turned up. Did the crew, seeing the schooner was going aground, take to the boats and drown? Were they picked up by the sulphur-laden *Hewitt,* which was known to be in the vicinity at the time, and later blew up, killing all aboard? Did modern-day pirates board her, kill the crew, and finding nothing of value aboard, run the vessel aground and abandon her? No one ever found out what did happen, and Captain Cat, who was adopted by one of the Hatterasmen, certainly never did tell.

JUGTOWN

JULIANA BUSBEE WALKED UP AND DOWN THE LONG ROWS OF EX-hibits at the county fair. It was in the autumn of 1915, and she had come to Lexington by train from her home in Raleigh to judge the cakes and jellies and fruits. It was a hot day and she was tired, and everything looked alike. Suddenly she stopped in her tracks, gazing at an exhibit of red apples piled one upon another. No, it was not the apples, it was the brilliant orange pie plate on which the apples were arranged. By Jove, what a beautiful plate!

Mrs. Busbee was a professional photographer with an artistic flair. She loved beautiful things. The bright orange glaze of the simple pie plate, its perfect roundness and design, held her motionless. Where did the pie plate come from? Could she buy others there in Lexington? "Oh," someone said, "what would you want with an ugly old dirt dish like that?" Yes, the local hardware store had some for sale. They were cheap, for nobody wanted dirt dishes.

As soon as she could, she hurried off to the hardware store and bought all that remained on the shelves at 10 cents apiece. The store got the pie plates, said the clerk, from somewhere down in the country. He really didn't know just where. He guessed some old-fashioned potter made them. There was not much sale for ugly dirt dishes.

Well, they might have been ugly to some people, but late that afternoon, Juliana Busbee sent her clothes home by mail. Then she carefully and lovingly packed the dirt dishes in her suitcase and returned home holding the suitcase in her lap all the way. Her heart almost jumped into her mouth at the thought that a shaking of the train or the stumbling of a passenger might jar her suitcase and break her precious 10-cent pie plates.

Back in Raleigh, she proudly showed the plates to her husband, Jacques Busbee, a portrait painter. He was as enthusiastic as she. "This is an old art, long almost forgotten," he said. "We must find the potter, wherever he is, and encourage him to continue his art." He looked again at the plates. "The most beautiful things are, after all, the simplest."

For months and months, Mr. and Mrs. Busbee looked for the mysterious potter who had made the brilliant orange pie plates. No one seemed to care about helping them in their search. Their friends in North Carolina thought that no homemade plates were as desirable as ones sent down from New York or across the ocean from Europe. But the Busbees were determined to find the potter and, if possible, to revive the ancient art.

Finally their search led them to an area in northwestern Moore County, about fifteen or twenty miles south of Asheboro. There, along the sand hills and among the piney woods, they located a group of older men who were turning out not only pie plates but also jugs, pitchers, crocks, pickle jars, churns, mugs, sugar bowls, and candlesticks. Some of the designs and glazes were beautiful like those of the orange pie plates.

One of the oldest of the men was called Josh Shuffle, though his real name was Josiah Wedgewood Sheffield. He knew a great deal about potters and potting. "Our fathers taught us how to make these dirt dishes," he explained. "First, we dig the clay from the clay pits hereabouts. We pick the gravel from it, then grind it in a mill that has a mule to turn it. When the clay is just right, we put some of it on a kick wheel." Juliana Busbee wanted to know what a kick wheel was.

"Well," Josh Shuffle said, "it's a turntable which goes round and round, and we keep it turning by pedaling or kicking with our feet, just the same as a woman pedals a sewing machine."

"But how do you shape the clay?" Mrs. Busbee asked.

"We mold the clay with our hands until we get a plate or a jar or whatever is needed. We use water to smooth it and dyes to color it. Later, all the pieces are stacked in a wood-burning kiln to bake."

"Everything is done by hand?" asked Jacques Busbee, remembering that almost all articles were then being made by machines. It was, he felt, the personal touch—that which

was done by a man himself and not by something else—
that made the pottery so different and so beautiful.

"Yes, everything," replied Josh Shuffle. "We make everything with our hands here."

By visiting other homes in the community, Mr. and Mrs.
Busbee found pieces of pottery, still being used, that were a
hundred or more years old. Much of the pottery was signed
and dated by various long-dead potters. Gradually the Busbees learned more. It seemed that about 1740 two potters
came from Staffordshire in England and settled in that very
part of North Carolina. With them, they brought their
knowledge of how to make pottery as it was made in England. The pottery of Staffordshire had been prized for
many, many generations.

In North Carolina the two potters had made no changes
in their technique. From father to son, the technique had
been passed down. Josh Shuffle was a direct descendant of
one of those two potters.

Thrilled by all they had learned, Juliana and Jacques
Busbee made a decision. They would give up their careers
as photographer and portrait painter, and they would de-
vote their lives to the revival of the art of pottery. It was
indeed to be a *revival,* for though the old techniques had
never died away, much of the current output was of poor
workmanship. Their only aim would be to preserve the
ancient tradition.

In May, 1917, with little or no money, the Busbees went
back to Moore County and began to build a log hut on a plot
of ground that they called Jugtown. Neither of the Busbees
planned to become a potter. They would live among the

potters, work with them, and teach them once again to respect the beauty of the ancient art. Jugtown was never a town or village but only a group of buildings dedicated to art.

Art is different from business, where making a profit is necessary. Money was to be of no importance at Jugtown. The advice of the Busbees to the potters was, "Take your time. Use the methods of your forefathers. It is a method known in olden times in China, Persia, and Egypt. Throw out any pot or plate that is not perfect."

The Moore County potters found that last bit of advice hard to take. Perfect or not, why not sell a jug for what one could get for it? The hard-working potters could not accept the principle that beauty alone was to be the criterion. Though they were glad the Busbees had come to help them, they wanted to turn out pottery fast and sell it quickly. They simply could not understand Jacques Busbee's scorn of money. They could not understand him when he said, "It is never how many jugs you can make in a day's time, but how beautiful each one is."

It is no wonder that, as the days passed, Jacques Busbee formed a new plan. Instead of working with the older men whose ways he could not change, he sought out young fellows with no experience but with, one might say, potting blood in their veins. One such young man was Ben Owen, son of the man who had made the orange pie plates that Juliana Busbee had seen in Lexington.

Ben Owen was a man of ability. With Mr. Busbee he went on a tour of the museums, where he observed superior examples of the potter's art from all countries and ages. Back at Jugtown, the two men studied over designs and glazes.

They hoped to improve the artistic quality of the pottery but to keep the technique. Every step in the production of a vase, for instance, was to be done by hand. Meanwhile, they developed new colors and shades. Besides bright orange and green, they created a dogwood white and a deep, deep tone that they called "Tobacco Spit Brown."

As the years passed, the Busbees enlarged their log house to seven rooms, and they trained more potters. Mrs. Busbee lived for a while in New York, where she opened a tea shop in which to display the Jugtown Ware, as it came to be known. Only after outsiders began to exclaim over Jugtown Ware and to buy it at the high prices the Busbees demanded did North Carolinians decide that Jugtown pottery was far more beautiful than the machine-manufactured pieces they had in their homes.

Even when success came to Jugtown, Jacques Busbee kept reminding his potters: "It is never how much work you do, or how much money it will bring you, but how much love and beauty you put into the thing you create."

Though the Busbees are now dead, there are many potters in the sandhill country who carry on the tradition. In the North Carolina Museum of Art in Raleigh are exhibited some of the best examples of Jugtown Ware.

YOUNG THOMAS WOLFE

NORTH CAROLINA HAS PRODUCED HUNDREDS OF WRITERS OF PO-
etry, plays, short stories, and novels. Among them, Thomas
Wolfe of Asheville is considered the greatest. Though Wolfe
wrote many books, he is best remembered for his novel of
over six hundred pages called *Look Homeward, Angel.*

He was born in Asheville, in the center of our western
North Carolina mountains, on October 3, 1900. His mother
was a mountain schoolteacher, and his father was a tomb-
stone cutter who had come south from Pennsylvania. At
his birth, Wolfe had two older sisters and four older
brothers.

Young Wolfe was smart. He was talking at the age of
one and reading a little bit by the time he was two years old.
Before he was four, his mother took all of the children to
the World's Fair in the faraway city of St. Louis on the
Mississippi River. Little Tom had a very good memory.

Even when he was grown, he remembered what the family did and where they went at the World's Fair in St. Louis. All these things he later wrote down in his first book, *Look Homeward, Angel.*

A month before his fifth birthday, he began the first grade at the Orange Street School in Asheville. His mother thought he was too young to stick it out, but Tom loved to read and became a good student.

By the time he was ready to enter the second grade, his mother bought a boarding house. There she rented rooms and served meals to people who had come to the mountains for a vacation. Tom talked to these people, listened carefully to what they had to say, and later put them in his stories.

Because he read his school books so quickly, he turned to his father's shelves for more reading. Also, he went to the public library for books. It seems that he never had enough to read.

In the afternoons after school, he sold magazines on the streets of Asheville to earn spending money, and when he was older, he had a newspaper route.

At Orange Street School, he made good grades. Once he won a spelling match because he was the only student in his school who could spell *asafetida.* His teachers were very proud of him. Two of them, Mr. and Mrs. J. M. Roberts, decided to start a private school, and the student they most wanted was Tom Wolfe, because he read more and wrote better than the other students. Tom's family was not rich, and sending him to the North State Fitting School would mean a lot of extra money, but at last his parents said that he could go.

Tom spent the last four years of high school in this private school with Mr. Roberts teaching him Latin and Greek and Mrs. Roberts teaching him English. Often Mrs. Roberts would take Tom aside to discuss books and poems with him. She helped him to improve his written work also, for she realized how talented he was. Someday, she thought, he may become a great writer! Once she became angry with Tom, because he could write and write and write without ever putting his sentences into paragraphs. On one of his papers, she noted: "I will never correct another one of your papers if you will not observe the rules of paragraphing!" This hard training was good for Tom. In his senior year, he won a prize for his long essay about the English poet William Shakespeare.

Now he was ready to go away to college, though he was not yet sixteen years old. His father wanted him to become a lawyer and offered to help pay the boy's expenses to the University of North Carolina at Chapel Hill. When young Wolfe arrived at the University, he was a strange sight. He was thin and tall—about six feet—with deep brown eyes, dark brown hair which he seldom combed, and enormous feet. The other students made fun of him as he loped along the campus paths. They did not know or care that this mountain boy had ability and promise.

During his sophomore year, Tom began to show them how wrong they had been. His stories and poems were being printed in the university *Magazine,* he became a member of the track team, and started being careful about combing his hair and wearing neat clothes. Tom Wolfe was becoming an important man on the campus. Instead of being laughed at, he was now admired by his fellow students.

By his junior year, he was taking his writing seriously. A new professor arrived in Chapel Hill to teach the writing of plays, and Tom was one of the first students to attend his class. He wrote short plays about the mountain people he had known in Asheville, and when they were acted on the stage of the Carolina Playmakers, Tom often took one of the parts himself.

In his last year at the University, he edited the student newspaper and wrote for other campus publications. He was on the Student Council and the Athletic Council. In fact, he was so busy with both his classroom work and his college activities that the school annual said jokingly of him: "He can do more between 8:25 and 8:30 than the rest of us can do all day, and it is no wonder that he is classed as a genius."

On graduation day in 1920, he was only nineteen years old, weighed 178 pounds, and was six feet and three inches tall. By now he had decided that he did not want to become a lawyer but wished, rather, to make writing his life work. So he went off to Harvard University for more study.

It was nine years later that his first novel, *Look Homeward, Angel,* was published. In this book, he wrote about a fellow named Eugene Gant, of how he grew up in a mountain town, and of how he went to the State University. Eugene Gant was really only another name for the author himself, and most of what happened in the book had happened to Thomas Wolfe.

Today, all over the world, his books are read and praised. In Asheville, one can visit not only his grave but also his mother's boarding house, where so many of the scenes in his first novel took place.

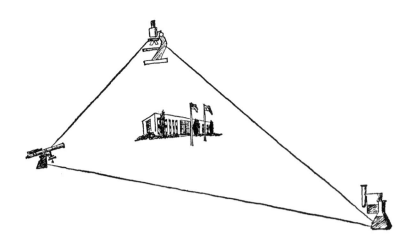

THE RESEARCH TRIANGLE PARK

IT STARTED AS A DREAM—AS ALL GREAT WORKS AND ACTIONS OF men have started. It started as a dream to put knowledge to work. If this could be done, every North Carolinian would be able to live a happier and more fruitful life.

For hundreds of years, agriculture was the main occupation of North Carolinians. After the Civil War, small mills began to dot the countryside, and sometimes they grew into large cotton, tobacco, or furniture factories. Following World War II, however, state leaders realized that agriculture and industry were only two of the three necessary ingredients of a balanced economy. The third one was scientific research. Agriculture and industry could thrive only when scholars and scientists were constantly seeking new ways to do things, discovering new knowledge to improve agriculture and industry, new knowledge to improve all of the ways of making a good living.

True, scientific research had not been entirely neglected in North Carolina. It had been carried on quietly by professors in the universities and by the trained technical men and women in the large manufacturing plants, but there was no *center* for research. After all, universities are busy teaching students, and manufacturing companies are busy making products to sell. A spot was needed where research was the only thing being done.

Again and again, this notion—this idea that many had dreamed of before—troubled the mind of Governor Luther H. Hodges. Most of the governors of North Carolina had been lawyers or farmers, but when Luther H. Hodges became governor, he brought to his office at the Capitol a different background. His life had been spent in industry. Because he had been connected with a large manufacturing corporation, he knew how important it was to discover new knowledge and to use it to improve whatever man was doing or making. Every manufacturer, every farmer, every doctor, every lawyer, and every teacher must always be looking for new ways of doing things. If he does not, he will soon find himself lagging behind. Governor Hodges was determined not to let North Carolina lag behind the other states.

Perhaps the dream might have remained just a dream that soon faded away but for a report that appeared in 1954. A committee of university professors from Durham, Chapel Hill, and Raleigh drew up a report about research in North Carolina's three largest universities: about what was being done, about what was not being done, and about what could be done if the three universities co-operated with each other. Governor Hodges was delighted. Would it not be possible, he thought, to use the vast resources of these three universities to begin a research triangle? The word *triangle* was an accurate one, because if a line is drawn on the map from Durham to Chapel Hill to Raleigh and back to Durham, a neat triangle is formed.

Governor Hodges talked to many prominent men about how to get the three universities to act as a single research team. Along with other problems that concerned him as governor, he thought of this frequently. No clear answer came to him, but he was so determined to have his dream come true that he set up a small office of workers to explore what might be done.

While these things were going on, some dark green rolling hills, covered with pines and oaks, were sleeping away in the sunshine and the rain just about an equal distance from the three campuses. Students drove over the rolling hills on their way to football games, professors rode past them on visits to one another, but no one looked upon the area as anything but a place to hunt birds among the pine trees on the ridges or to seine for minnows in the little branches that flowed in the ravines. It was beautiful land, almost deserted except for the highways and railroads bordering and crossing it.

Suddenly, while Governor Hodges' men were looking here and there to see where they could find a place to set up a center for scientific research, they heard that a thousand acres of this very land was for sale. Moving cautiously, Governor Hodges asked some wealthy men, who were eager to do something special for North Carolina, to purchase the tract, with the plan that it would later become the Research Triangle Park.

Why a park? Why not build a town and put the research buildings in the middle of the town? No! From the beginning, it was decided that North Carolina's Research Triangle Park, unique in that it was the first place in the United States to be *planned* from the start as a research park, was to be located where there was much open space. Towns, with busy, cluttered streets, naturally are noisy, but out in the woods, in a well-kept park, quiet prevails. Man thinks and dreams better in a quiet atmosphere, and the park was to be a "breeding place for ideas," a spot where man could think up new ways of doing things.

Other tracts of adjoining land were added to the original thousand acres, and soon there were five thousand acres—a big park indeed. The men who had bought the land at the Governor's request wished, as soon as possible, to turn over the land at cost to the nonprofit Research Triangle Foundation. During the early months of 1959, in a campaign that lasted only sixty days, a sum of more than a million and a half dollars was raised from businesses and public-spirited individuals to purchase the land, improve it, and put the Triangle to work. Governor Hodges was kept busy inviting various agencies from government and private business to buy land in the park and then to erect buildings in which scientific research could be carried on.

At this point, the Research Triangle Institute was organized. If a public or private organization wanted to have research done on a certain scientific problem, but did not want to put up a building and employ a permanent staff of workers, the organization engaged the Institute to do the research. Soon the Institute, with its own roster of trained scientists, was busy carrying on research in all sorts of areas: physics, biology, mathematics, agriculture, forestry, engineering, and other fields. For special researchers, the Institute called on the faculties of the three universities.

The Institute, satisfactory as it was for limited projects, could not, and was not expected to, handle large, long-term research problems. In a short while, handsome buildings were erected in the park for the purpose of pursuing one kind of research on a continuing basis. The first privately owned business to come to the park was an important American manufacturing firm that wanted a quiet spot, away from its other activities, to do research in chemical fibers. More private businesses followed. Then the United States government chose the park for an insect and disease laboratory and also as a center to study environmental health sciences. Another kind of nationwide activity to erect a building in the park, but not sponsored by the United States government, was the American Association of Textile Chemists and Colorists, which decided the park was an excellent spot for its laboratory and scientific library. An example on the state level is the North Carolina Science and Technology Research Center, whose purpose is to make it possible for the industries of the state to "contribute to and benefit from the economic and technical advancements in the Age of Space."

As a matter of fact, there is simply no kind of scientific research that some part of the Triangle is not able to undertake. For, it must be remembered, the Triangle is not one thing alone, not one place by itself. It is three counties: Durham, Orange, and Wake. It is three cities: Durham, Chapel Hill, and Raleigh. It is three universities: Duke University, the University of North Carolina at Chapel Hill, and North Carolina State University, with all of their scholars and laboratories ready to be used when needed. And it is all the various agencies within the park itself.

All of these numerous elements go to make up the Triangle. It is no wonder that the Triangle has brought fame to North Carolina. It has stimulated industrial research. It has attracted to the state business organizations that consider it necessary to be located near a research center. Such organizations are always of a high type, employing mostly college graduates, and paying top salaries. Though the Triangle has meant much to North Carolina, it has not been financed by tax dollars but by the willing contributions of loyal citizens who wanted to improve the living conditions of all Tar Heels everywhere.

Governor Hodges worked closely with the Triangle in its beginning days—asking for money to support it, entertaining companies who might locate in it, doing whatever was necessary. Then, for four years, starting in 1961, he lived in Washington, D.C., while he was Secretary of Commerce by appointment of President John F. Kennedy. When he retired from official public life, he returned to North Carolina and once more took up the cause of the Triangle, knowing now that dreams come true, but knowing too that dreams will fade unless much work goes into keeping them bright and prosperous and real.

Headquarters of the Research Triangle Park is the Hanes Building, named for Robert M. Hanes of Winston-Salem, one of the first men to foresee, with Governor Hodges, the greatness of the Research Triangle concept. A visitor to the park always begins his tour at the Hanes Building.

BATTLESHIP

SHE IS A BEAUTIFUL SIGHT—THE BATTLESHIP *North Carolina.*
After an exciting life, she now rests quietly in a berth especially prepared for her across the Cape Fear River from
the busy streets of Wilmington. A poet wrote of her:

> Long live the *North Carolina!*
> She never knew defeat.
> The foe six times announced her sunk,
> But still she led the fleet!

This proud "Showboat" of the United States Navy, which
once gave its most powerful ships the names of the various
states, was not the first to be so called. The first *North
Carolina* was a 74-gun frigate that sailed the seas early in
our history. The second was a cruiser, used in transport

duty during World War I. Later, when the Navy designed a ship to be mightier than any the world had ever seen, she would be the third *North Carolina.*

After three years' building at the New York Navy Yard, she was launched in 1940 by the Governor's daughter, Miss Isabel Hoey, with these words: "In the name of the United States, I christen thee *North Carolina.*"

What a battleship! She was 728 feet long, much over twice the length of a football field, and 108 feet at the beam. Behind her 16-inch steel belt, she carried 2,500 officers and men—enough people to fill up a whole town—and had four airplanes aboard. She had cost the United States government $76,885,750. Her chief glory, however, was her firing power. Her 16-inch guns, the largest afloat, could hit a target 22 miles away. It is no wonder that she was called the "Showboat."

She had been built just in time. Six months after the United States and Japan declared war on each other in 1941, the *North Carolina* slipped down the Atlantic coast and passed through the Panama Canal. At Pearl Harbor, in Hawaii, she learned that her main job would be the protection of the fast Navy aircraft carriers. She was badly needed, as the United States was poorly prepared for the war. When the *North Carolina* joined the Pacific Fleet, she was almost the only big ship there. She was the first big *new* ship in the Pacific, and she stayed there until victory was won.

In three years of fighting, she was a lucky lady. In at least fifty brushes with the Japanese, in which nine men were killed and forty-four wounded, she received no crippling damage. She now sports twelve battle stars for her twelve major engagements. At six different times, the Japanese reported her sunk, but the proud *North Carolina* simply would not be sent to the bottom of the ocean.

Her first great battle came on August 24, 1942, at five o'clock in the afternoon, when she was protecting the aircraft carrier *Enterprise*. About fifteen Japanese planes came over, hit the *Enterprise* with their bombs, then attacked the *North Carolina*. Suddenly forty-four more enemy planes shot out of the distance. They swooped down on the "Showboat," but she was lucky. Though a Japanese gun killed one sailor, there was no direct bomb-hit on the battleship. Meanwhile, the *North Carolina* gunners shot down seven Japanese planes.

Three weeks later, she had her worst moment. A torpedo, which was fired from an enemy submarine, hit her in the side and tore a hole, 32 by 18 feet, in her 16-inch steel belt. Five *North Carolina* sailors were killed, but the ship kept on course, fighting as she went.

After many more battles, she steamed into Tokyo Bay in 1945 for the surrender of the Japanese. Then she turned around and began the happiest voyage of her life, for the war was over and she was coming home.

In spite of the glorious record of the mighty, victorious, lucky "Showboat," her future looked sad. With the invention of rockets and missiles, the *North Carolina* was too slow and had too little firing power to compete in a Jet Age. She would be an easy target for the new weapons of war, so the Navy decided to take her out of service, to "put her in moth balls," as the saying goes. For many years, she lay in her berth in New Jersey, no sailors walking her decks. Then in 1961, the Navy announced she would be sold for junk.

On learning the news, North Carolinians grew angry. Sell their proud namesake for junk! What could they do to save her? The United States government told our Governor that the state could have the *North Carolina,* if plans could be made to tow her away from the New Jersey berth. Right away, North Carolinians started collecting money. Soon they had $345,000, a fourth of it given by 700,000 school children who brought in nickels and dimes. It was enough, and the *North Carolina* was saved from disgrace in a junk-yard. She would be brought to Wilmington and preserved as a memorial to all Tar Heels who died in battle during World War II.

On an autumn day in 1961, seven tugs moved the *North Carolina* out into the harbor from her New Jersey dock. Ships in the harbor saluted with their horns and whistles as she slipped out to sea. Once out in the Atlantic Ocean, five of the boats moved aside, leaving two sea-going tugs to pull her down the coast. On the huge *North Carolina,* which now had no power of her own, rode five men. On the fifth day, the two little tugs with their mighty battleship arrived at the mouth of the Cape Fear River. The next day, with thousands of North Carolina citizens lining the banks of the river, the "Showboat" eased her way up the river to Wilmington. Captain B. M. Burriss of Southport, who knew every sandbar in the bed of the Cape Fear, was the pilot. He moved her along slowly, the largest ship ever to float on the waves of the river.

Things went well until she arrived at Wilmington. Then, turning into her berth, the *North Carolina* jammed a hole in a floating restaurant on the Wilmington side of the river. Her bow went aground on the opposite shore. Quickly, eleven tugs went into action, a bulldozer on land got hold of her, and after thirty minutes she was free and was moved into her permanent home.

There she is today—the great proud ship! Visitors climb over her spare anchor, go up and down her ladders, jump into the same gun-mounts from which the enemy was once destroyed, and steer her from the bridge. They go deep down into her lower decks, where the sailors slept and ate, and can sit in the officers' ward room. They can even mail a post card at the first rural post office ever put aboard a battleship.

There is little evidence of her battle damage. A dent is on her port side, a nick in her superstructure, but nothing to show where the Japs put a huge hole in her.

The greatest moment for the visitor to the *North Carolina,* which is open every day of the week, is that moment when he stands high up on the battleship and imagines he is steaming toward the enemy at twenty-eight knots.

In summertime, a nightly "Sound and Light" performance tells the dramatic story of "The Immortal Showboat" in flame and smoke and thunder. A small fee is charged for the hour-long performance.

OLD CHRISTMAS

CHRISTMAS COMES TWICE A YEAR AT RODANTHE, A TINY VILLAGE
on the Outer Banks at the north end of Hatteras Island. The
citizens of Rodanthe like it that way, and the children love
it. First, they have the same Christmas as everybody else
on December 25. Then, eleven days later, they have what
they call Old Christmas. It is said that nowhere else in the
United States, except at Rodanthe, is Old Christmas still
celebrated.

December 25 comes to Rodanthe in the usual way. The
schools have closed down, stockings are hung near the chimney in the sitting room, and Santa Claus fills them for the
younger children on Christmas Eve. On Christmas day,
presents are given, and a big Christmas dinner is served.
The only difference is Rodanthe itself, where the Atlantic
Ocean rolls up noisily on the white beach, and a bitterly
cold wind, the nor'easter, may be howling down the sandbanks and shaking the windows and doors of the fishermen's
houses. A really bad storm may bring angry waves almost
up to the front steps of the houses.

The traditional date for Old Christmas is January 5. In early times, before the highway was built to Rodanthe, the villagers gathered together at daybreak for a parade. In front were two men, one playing a fife, the other beating a drum. Then came the Sunday School choir, followed by the rest of the Rodanthe folks. Trudging through the sand, they marched to Waves, a village a mile to the south, where they had many friends. From house to house they went, playing their instruments and singing before each house to wake up the sleepers. During the rest of the morning, the boys and men played ball games on the sand, and the girls and women visited in the homes. At noon, a picnic was held. In the evening, everyone gathered at the Rodanthe one-room schoolhouse for singing and acting out little plays.

Then came the big moment: the appearance of Old Buck. Old Buck was a wild bull from the pine forests at the southern tip of Hatteras Island, and a terrible creature he was. He entered onto the stage from the back door of the schoolhouse. For a while he stood there, snorting and prancing and looking out over the audience. The small children were greatly afraid of Old Buck, for he had come to punish them for the bad things they had done during the year. They were afraid of him even though they knew he was not really a wild bull but two men under a blanket, with a cow's head and horns at the front.

Suddenly Old Buck jumped from the platform and roared at the children on the front rows. While the girls shrank from him, the boys leaped from their seats to attack the monster. They knew that Old Buck had come to destroy the Spirit of Christmas, and this they were determined he should not do. Hitting him on the right and on the left, they finally drove him from the schoolhouse. The Spirit of Christmas had been saved for another year!

After the defeat of Old Buck, the benches were moved back and a square dance started. Late at night, all the villagers returned to their homes, tired and sleepy, thinking sadly that Old Christmas would not come for another twelve months.

When the highway was paved down the sandbanks, it looked as if the villagers of Rodanthe—now no longer cut off from the mainland—would give up their merrymaking on January 5 and celebrate only on December 25 like everybody else. After all, some people argued, there was no reason why Rodanthe should keep its Old Christmas. One celebration of Christmas was enough, they said. But, in spite of these arguments, Old Christmas was not abandoned. Today, it is a time of homecoming at Rodanthe, when those who have moved away return to visit their relatives and friends. Often, instead of January 5, Old Christmas is celebrated on any early Saturday in January, when it is convenient for people to come back to this village by the side of the ocean.

Today, on the Saturday night set aside for the celebration, the Christmas trees are brightly lighted at Rodanthe. Christmas decorations hang in the windows of all the homes. A parade is held in the afternoon, with the people riding in automobiles instead of trudging across the sand. After the parade, a barbecue and an oyster roast are held, the ocean winds sweeping the hot flames in the oyster pit higher than a man's head. At dark, everybody gathers in the schoolhouse, just as in the past. Songs are sung, and little plays are acted out.

And then comes the big moment: the appearance of Old Buck, just as he has come every January at Rodanthe. The drum is beating furiously—the same drum that has been in use a hundred years. Old Buck, to the beat of the drum, leaps about the stage, then comes down into the audience. As in the past, the tiny children pretend to be afraid of him, but finally they leap from their seats and chase him from the building. The Spirit of Christmas has been saved! The Spirit of Christmas must never, never be defeated! Old Buck must wait another year to try once more.

When told about Old Christmas, everybody wants, of course, to know how it came about. It started because of a change in the calendar we now use. Long ago it was discovered that the old calendar was not accurate, that it was longer than the full year as determined by the four seasons. To make things right for once and all, the American colonists in 1752 dropped eleven days out of September. Such a change put December 25 eleven days earlier than in the year before.

Though the colonists slowly accepted the new calendar, some people said the "real" Christmas was not on December 25 any longer but on January 5. They said they would continue to celebrate the birth of Christ on the "old" day, regardless of what month it came in, and so they did.

Gradually, however, almost everybody in America forgot about the "real" Christmas day and the old calendar. Almost everybody, that is, except in the village of Rodanthe. The folks in Rodanthe, living there on the lonely sandbanks, were once so cut off from the towns and cities of the mainland that they kept to their old customs. The time came, however, when some of the young villagers decided on the new December 25 date, but the older citizens would not give up January 5. Rather than quarrel about which date was *really* correct, the Rodanthe fishermen and their families decided they would have two Christmases.

They thought that if one Christmas was a good thing, two Christmases would be twice as good. It would be well, said some of the wise older people, if on every day of the year, Old Buck could be beaten back and the Spirit of Christmas celebrated in the lives of us all.

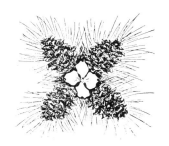